Philosophy and the Art o

Philosophy and literature enjoy a close, complex relationship. Elucidating the connections between these two fields, this book examines the ways philosophy deploys literary means to advance its practice, particularly as a way of life that extends beyond literary forms and words into physical deeds, nonlinguistic expression, and subjective moods and feelings.

Exploring thinkers from Socrates and Confucius to Foucault and Simone de Beauvoir, Richard Shusterman probes the question of what roles literature could play in a vision of philosophy as something essentially lived rather than merely written. To develop this vision of philosophy that incorporates literature but seeks to go beyond the verbal to realize the embodied fullness of life and capture its inexpressible dimensions, Shusterman gives particular attention to authors who straddle the literature/philosophical divide: from Augustine and Montaigne through Wordsworth and Kierkegaard to T.S. Eliot, Georges Bataille, Maurice Blanchot, and Bertrand Russell. The book concludes with a chapter on the Chinese art of writing with its mixture of poetry, calligraphy, and painting.

Philosophy and the Art of Writing should interest students and researchers in literary theory and philosophy. It also opens the practice of philosophy to people who are not professionals in the writing of philosophy or literary theory.

Richard Shusterman is the Dorothy F. Schmidt Eminent Scholar in the Humanities at Florida Atlantic University, USA, where he is also Professor of Philosophy and English, and Director of the Center for Body, Mind, and Culture.

New Literary Theory
Series editors: Andy Mousley and Jeff Wallace

Just Literature
Philosophical Criticism and Justice
Tzachi Zamir

Happiness
Jeffrey R. Di Leo

Philosophy and the Art of Writing
Richard Shusterman

For more information about this series, please visit: www.routledge.com/New-Literary-Theory/book-series/NLTH

Philosophy and the Art of Writing

Richard Shusterman

Routledge
Taylor & Francis Group
LONDON AND NEW YORK

First published 2022
by Routledge
4 Park Square, Milton Park, Abingdon, Oxon OX14 4RN

and by Routledge
605 Third Avenue, New York, NY 10158

Routledge is an imprint of the Taylor & Francis Group, an informa business

British Library Cataloguing-in-Publication Data
A catalogue record for this book is available from the British Library

Library of Congress Cataloging-in-Publication Data
A catalog record has been requested for this book

ISBN: 978-0-367-35490-9 (hbk)
ISBN: 978-1-032-23080-1 (pbk)
ISBN: 978-0-429-33177-0 (ebk)

DOI: 10.4324/9780429331770

Typeset in Sabon
by Deanta Global Publishing Services, Chennai, India

For Teddy

Contents

Series Preface viii
Preface x

1 Philosophy and Literature: The Quarrels of Intimacy 1

2 Writing, Identity, and the Unity of Self 23

3 Expressing the Ineffable 58

4 The Art of Writing in Chinese Thought 92

Works Cited 121
Index 128

Series Preface

Why does or should literature matter to us? What is its value and significance for human existence in the twenty-first century? *New Literary Theory* aims to breathe new life into the way we think about literature. The books in the series will be erudite but not narrowly specialist, informed by up-to-date research but not overburdened by scholarly reference. The spirit of the series is to emulate the vitality, experimentalism and freedom of literature itself, and to find fresh and accessible ways of writing about our engagements with it.

The re-focusing of attention upon the particularities of literature is not intended to be nostalgic or defensive. The series will encourage a plurality of approaches to 'the literary' and will not seek to prescribe what literary studies now is or might become in an era of revolutionary cultural transformation in which the conditions for reading texts as 'literature' are drastically changing, if not disappearing. For 'literature' consists not simply in its sources of value – works of art and their creators – but in the reading formations and institutions that make the concept of literature possible: textual literacy; the possibility of the individual's sustained, private encounter with the text, or time and space to read in an undistracted way; an educational system in which to teach the concept of the literary. Books, the market activists tell us, are still alive and well; but are their readers still out there and, if so, for how long? The reorientation of human consciousness in 'developed' societies and the monopolisation of attention and concentration through digital technology, screens, mobile phones and social media is occurring with extraordinary rapidity.

Our rationale for reinvigorating and re-imagining the literary is in part provoked by the implications of these far-reaching cultural changes. But it can simultaneously be traced back to the historical and conceptual drift between 'literary theory' and the thing that became 'theory'. The revolution in literary studies from the 1960s onwards was fired by an initial interest in the theory of what literature is and does, gathered from various twentieth-century sources – from, say, Russian formalism, through New Criticism, stylistics, structuralism and narratology to post-structuralism. But then 'theory' detached itself, becoming no longer simply a concern with the literary as such, but a way of reading literature in and through philosophy, psychology and psychoanalysis, movements of political thought and activism, and frameworks of ethical value. The series will build upon each of these aspects of 'literary/theory', acknowledging their immeasurable enrichment of literary studies as a mode of intellectual work. Yet we are also eager to (re)focus attention on what it means to think concertedly 'with literature' about any given field of enquiry.

There has been a tendency, also, for the teaching of literary theory in undergraduate programmes to become routinised, with undergraduate modules delivering literary theory as a 'toolkit' of critical approaches which bleach out the historical contexts or political motivations and struggles behind such approaches. The perceived obligation to master and deploy literary-theoretical languages did, inevitably, lead to new kinds of professional performance in critical writing, perhaps sometimes neglectful of the need to keep what was once called, most notably by Virginia Woolf, the intelligent 'common reader', alert and awake. In this sense the academicisation of theory could seem to be at odds with its emancipatory promise. Resistance to such tendencies means trying to assimilate theory with those more 'common' terms in which readers and students might want to register their engagements with literary texts – emotion and evaluation, perplexity and enlightenment, loving and hating.

Andy Mousley and Jeff Wallace

Preface

This book is a brief study of the relationship between literature and philosophy, more particularly a study of the use of literature for a particular form of philosophy. It bears witness to the extensive overlap between philosophy and literature, and to the error of assuming a deep and necessary divide between them. If the distinction between these fields is difficult to draw in a clear, decisive way, then the line between philosophy and literary theory seems even harder to define. Despite the vagueness and porosity of their borders, this book argues for a distinction between philosophy and literature (including literary theory), while conversely arguing for literature's priceless contribution to philosophy. Philosophy is more than literature and literary theory, because it is more than language. It is more than language because its love and quest of wisdom is not merely a verbal affair; it is a way of life.

The philosophical life cannot be merely verbal because wisdom involves embodied deeds and affective attitudes toward life; we cannot reduce wisdom to a set of wise truths or sayings, because it requires wise ways of feeling and acting in the world. Its most powerful expressions may not be expressions of great verbal power and may not be verbal at all. Although literary theory cannot fully capture this more-than-verbal, lived dimension of philosophy, it should acknowledge this dimension while equally recognizing how literature, including philosophical literature, deploys its qualities of verbal artistry to promote philosophy's more-than-verbal quest for wisdom. Hence, *Philosophy and the Art of Writing* seems to me a fitting title for this book on the uses of writing for the philosophical life.

The book's first chapter traces the ancient roots of the border disputes between philosophy and literature through philosophy's struggle to establish its intellectual dominance as the superior source of wisdom. The chapter then examines the most prominent ways theorists have tried to distinguish the two fields: linguistically, logically, and ultimately through the idea of philosophy as an art of living that seeks wisdom through self-knowledge and self-improvement with ethical concern for others. This concept of the philosophical life was very prominent in the ancient world and still survives in contemporary times, although largely eclipsed by philosophy's current, narrow self-image as an academic profession. The chapter then explores the different ways that literature's art of writing is essential for the success of philosophy as a life practice focused on such aims as self-knowledge, self-cultivation, and care for the self and others, despite the fact that these aims involve dimensions that are nonlinguistic and hence nonliterary.

The second chapter turns from these more general arguments to the detailed analysis of how four key thinkers make the art of writing essential to their art of living and quest for self-knowledge, self-improvement, and wisdom: Augustine, Montaigne, Wordsworth, and Kierkegaard. Spanning the cultures of antiquity, the Renaissance, Romanticism, and modernity, these writers also straddle the presumed divide between philosophy and literature. Chapter 3 focuses on the subtle ways that literature's artful writing can communicate dimensions of reality and experience (and even wisdom) that ordinary language and standard philosophical discourse cannot express. Here we examine the theory and practice of four great twentieth-century writers – Georges Bataille, Maurice Blanchot, T.S. Eliot, and Bertrand Russell – who show some surprising affinities in their views despite their stylistic differences and who likewise defy pigeonholing as belonging only to literature or only to philosophy.

The book's final chapter departs from its Eurocentric focus to consider China's classical pursuit of the philosophical life through the art of writing. This involves a study of the Chinese technique of writing with the brush that defines its calligraphic tradition and whose extension of writing into the pictorial form of ink wash painting combines with calligraphy and poetry to create what the Chinese regard as the artistry of "the three perfections." This art of writing also created the figure of the scholar-theorist-poet-painter, whose philosophical quest for self-knowledge and self-cultivation involves a form of literature that is more than merely verbal and conceptual because of the painterly qualities of calligraphy and pictorial brushwork. These aesthetic skills of the brush imply certain somaesthetic skills and training that nourish the philosophical art of living. I examine this augmented writing of "three perfections" in six important works by four famous Chinese masters who stretch from the thirteenth to the sixteenth century. This final chapter allows us to examine the somatic and material dimensions of the art of writing that literary theory and the philosophy of literature have largely neglected.

Because this book belongs to a series whose format requires narrow limits of length, I have had to condense many arguments and to omit many examples and references that would otherwise be appropriate. I hope readers will forgive this. The series bears the title "New Literary Theory," yet none of the theorists on whom I focus could qualify as new. If there is genuine novelty in this book, it resides in its somaesthetic approach to the art of writing, its juxtaposition of authors, and its consideration of the philosophical import of China's rich tradition of calligraphic literature. Could there also be novelty in providing fresh reminders of important old ideas that theory's current fashions have obscured or neglected, for example the ancient idea of the philosophical life, of philosophy as an art of living? In any case, rather than straining for novelty, this book aims to be engagingly instructive. Above all, as a philosopher and a writer, I seek to be honest. Committed to the philosophical life, in theory and practice, I acknowledge this book belongs to that life.

***

For the past 16 years I have enjoyed the generous support of the Schmidt Family Foundation whose philanthropy established the Dorothy F. Schmidt Eminent Scholar Chair in the Humanities at Florida Atlantic University, which I am honored to hold. This book provides another occasion to express my profound gratitude to the Schmidts. I thank my FAU colleague Ken Holloway, the Levenson Professor of Asian Studies at FAU, and Dr. Gao Yanping of the Literature Institute of the Chinese Academy of Social Sciences (Beijing) for helpful comments on the book's China chapter. John Golden and Stéphane Madelrieux have my thanks for bibliographical help regarding Wordsworth and Bataille, as do my doctoral students Gabriella Piconi, Megan Spring, and T.J. Bonnet for their skill and dedication in tracking down references when library restrictions due to COVID-19 made such tasks especially difficult. I gratefully acknowledge permission to revise and expand some arguments from Chapter 3 relating to Bertrand Russell and from Chapter 4 relating to Chinese calligraphy that I provisionally proposed, respectively, in the journal *Modern Fiction Studies* and in the edited volume *Transformative Aesthetics*, published by Routledge. I thank editors Andy Mousley and Jeff Wallace for inviting me to write a book for this series and for encouraging me to complete this task more expeditiously and concisely than I anticipated.

1 Philosophy and Literature: The Quarrels of Intimacy

Ancient Roots of a Struggle for Distinction and Dominance

Philosophy and literature enjoy an extremely old, richly intimate but also problematic relationship. Already Plato could speak of an ancient "quarrel between philosophy and poetry" (Plato *Republic* Book X, 607b 1969).[1] In literary theory, the connection is especially intimate and complex as the borders with philosophy are very hard to demarcate. Plato's critique of poetry in the *Republic* is the foundational text of literary theory, yet given its dialogue form, its storytelling, and its imaginative and stylistic qualities, the *Republic* is also a literary work itself, just as it is undeniably philosophy.

Philosophy is often conceived primarily in terms of definitional "what is?" questions, such as what is knowledge, what is justice, what is beauty? From that perspective, philosophy of literature should take as its initial task the definition of literature; and this implies that it should examine the nature of literature with objective, critical distance. But if philosophy is itself a form of literature, is this external perspective really possible? And how can we convincingly deny that philosophy is, in some sense, literature, given the enormous breadth of the concept of literature? We cannot exclude philosophy from literature by reducing literature to fictional discourse since much literature is nonfictional and aims at truth. Philosophy, moreover, displays a variety of recognized literary genres: essays, dialogues, poems, meditations, treatises, speeches, confessions, memoirs, letters, discourses, journals, commentaries, investigations, sermons, notes, lectures, fragments, aphorisms, inquiries, outlines, and sketches. We could easily extend this list, which will continue to grow with new literary forms like the blog, which has already found wide philosophical use.

We cannot argue that philosophy is not literature by claiming that some ancient philosophers (including Socrates) never wrote any philosophical texts but only communicated their views in oral dialogue. Even if the term "literature" derives from the Latin root for "letter" and thus suggests writing, the concept of literature clearly includes oral literature. Indeed, ancient Greek poetry was essentially intended for oral transmission and was preserved through oral tradition before being committed to textual form. To

DOI: 10.4324/9780429331770-1

award philosophy the privilege of defining literature while recognizing that literature is the subsuming genus that includes philosophical discourse as one of its species would suggest a logically disconcerting circularity. Even if we dismiss concerns of circularity, philosophy seems compelled to cede literature the status of generic primacy. Philosophers, however, have rarely been willing to concede this, perhaps because of philosophy's traditional proud rivalry and embarrassed sense of belatedness. Philosophy first emerged as a major force in ancient Greece by asserting its superiority to poetry and rhetoric as a better source not only of truth for the conduct of life but also for the highest kind of beauty and happiness.

With Socrates and Plato, philosophy was born of a struggle for intellectual supremacy fought against the rhetoricians or sophists on the one hand and the artists on the other. Poetry was the prime artistic enemy, since it best captured the sacred wisdom of tradition and lacked the banausic character of plastic art. As philosophy adapted many of rhetoric's strategies of argumentation, so it took key epistemological and metaphysical orientations from art. The ideal of knowledge as *theoria* (which means detached contemplation of reality rather than reconstructive interaction with it) reflects the attitude of a spectator at a drama or an appreciative observer of a finely finished work of plastic art or poetry. Similarly, the idea that reality ultimately consists of well-defined and stable *forms* that are rationally and harmoniously ordered and whose contemplation affords sublime pleasure suggests a preoccupation with fine works of art, an envious fixation on their clear, purposive, well-wrought forms and distinct contours, their enduring and intelligible harmonies that set them above the confusing flux of ordinary experience. This makes art seem more vivid, permanent, compelling – in a sense more *real* – than ordinary empirical reality. Since the poets were highly esteemed not only as creators of beauty but also as purveyors of wisdom, philosophy had to establish its autonomy and privilege by defining poetry, drama, and other fine arts in more negative terms. With keen dialectical ingenuity, it transformed its imitations of art into a depreciative definition of art as imitation, or *mimesis* (Plato *Republic* 595a–607b).

For Plato, not only was art (as imitation of mere appearance) twice removed from the true forms of reality, not only did it deceive and appeal to the lowest part of the soul, but it also could not compete with philosophy in terms of beauty and the pleasures of desire. While art might provide a view of beautiful objects, philosophy could offer the rapt contemplation of the more perfect transcendental forms that make art's imitative objects (and indeed all objects) beautiful, providing a program of visionary delectation culminating in the ultimate beauty and object of desiring love, the very form of Beauty itself. Plato therefore describes the philosopher as not only the expert on wisdom but also "the master of the art of love" (Plato *Symposium* 198d 1997: 481). In short, Plato defined art not to promote its practice or enhance its appreciative understanding, but rather to deprecate, confine, and control it – even to the extent of censorship and banishment.

The critique of poetry as inferior to philosophy pervades Plato's dialogues. In the *Apology*, Socrates relates that after he found the politicians wanting in wisdom because they thought they knew things they did not really know, he "went to the poets" and found that they could not properly explain the meaning of "the poems they themselves had composed" (Plato *Apology* 22b 1966a). He concluded that "they composed [their works] not by wisdom, but by nature and because they were inspired, like the prophets and givers of oracles; for these also say many fine things, but know none of the things they say" (22c). Yet, "on account of their poetry, [they] thought that they were the wisest of men in other things as well, in which they were not" (22c). The dialogue *Ion* extends this critique of literature as radically remote from knowledge by explaining both poetic composition and reception as irrational, albeit divinely inspired, madness (or *mania*). Ion's prize-winning talent as an interpretive reciter of Homer's poetry derives not from real knowledge or "mastery" but from "a divine power" from the Muses, which first inspires Homer and then extends from him through Ion and all the way to the appreciative listeners that thrill to Ion's recitations (Plato *Ion* 532c–534b 1997: 942). Socrates likens this to a magnetic chain of inspiration, where the "poets utter all those fine poems not from art [*techne* or skilled knowledge] but as inspired and possessed" and thus essentially out of their minds (Plato *Ion* 533e 1925a). No poet can properly compose "until he has been inspired and put out of his senses, and his mind is no longer in him" (Plato *Ion* 534b 1925a). In the *Phaedrus*, Plato reaffirms this theory of poetic creation and experience as a "kind of possession and madness [that] comes from the Muses": "he who without the divine madness comes to the doors of the Muses, confident that he will be a good poet by art, meets with no success, and the poetry of the sane man vanishes into nothingness before that of the inspired madmen" (Plato *Phaedrus* 245a 1925b).

In this critique of poetry's irrational frenzy, the worry is not simply lack of knowledge, but the loss of a strong, autonomous, rationally moderate self who exemplifies the ideals of excellent character, sound mind, and self-control that belong to the ancient Greek virtue of *sophrosyne*, deemed essential to wisdom. If Socrates defined philosophy's quest through the Delphic injunction "Know Thyself" and understood this as knowing one's mind, then what could be worse than losing your mind and self-control through possession by a foreign force, even if divine? The ancient Greeks prized the manly values of autonomy and independence that found expression in their political structure of independent city-states and in their ideals of heroism, athleticism, and virile dominance. Sexually, it was admirable for a man to penetrate but shameful to be penetrated, because the latter implied a passive, subordinate, feminized role of being possessed by another. Even within the Greek culture of male pederasty, penetration by one's lover carried a hint of disgrace, of being weak and womanly; even if permitted, it should not be enjoyed, but instead only tolerated as an expression of the beloved's affectionate submission to the older lover's desire.[2] If sexual penetration of one's body by another was a shameful thing for any noble male (no matter how worthy the penetrator), then one could easily understand how penetration and possession of one's psyche would appear extremely threatening, even if that other was divine. Plato's word for poetic "inspiration" in *Ion* is ἔνθεοι whose etymology suggests being penetrated, full of, or possessed by a god (Plato *Ion* 533e 1925a). Defining the poet as a being irrationally possessed or penetrated by another served to gender poetry as an essentially feminized practice, characterized by weakness and lack of control, and thus removed from the masculine ideals of Greek virtue.

This worry concerning effeminate weakness pervades Plato's critique of literature in his *Republic*. It complements the other, perhaps more famous charges this dialogue makes against poetry, drama, and the arts in general: that they are inferior and deceptive imitations of appearances rather than presenting true knowledge of the ultimate forms of reality, and thus they are not worthy of serious attention. As "poetry, and in general the mimetic art ... is far removed from truth" and is at best "a form of play, not to be taken seriously," so it also presents contents that "are both impious and false" (Plato *Republic* Book III 391e; Book X 602b–603a 1969). But this, Plato claims, is not the "chief accusation against [poetry]," which instead is "its power to corrupt" by stimulating and fostering "the inferior part of the soul" that enjoys emotions and irrational, self-indulgent, unserious, and unmanly behavior, whether of tragic "lamentations" or comic "buffooneries" (Book X 605a, 605c, 606c; Book III 387d). Even Homer's poetic passages are dangerous because "the more poetic they are the less are they suited to the ears of boys and men" who should be strong, brave, and self-controlled (Book III 387b). Literature's emotional depictions of the terrors of war and the pleasures of love and "bodily appetites" tend to "make [men] more sensitive and soft than we would have them" (Book III 387c, 389e). Such scenes "certainly are not suitable for youth to hear for the inculcation of self-control" and the proper "conduct of a man [instead of] ... that of a woman" (Book III 390a; Book X 605e).[3]

Plato attacks literature from another angle in the *Phaedrus* by radically arguing that writing itself (whether or not poetic or fictional) is simply inadequate for doing the serious business of philosophy. Writing involves multiple problems. It weakens the minds of those who use it "because they will not practice their memory" (Plato *Phaedrus* 275a 1925b). Moreover, it makes readers and writers conceitedly "hard to get along with," thinking they really know and have in active memory the things they have read and written, when in fact "they are not wise" (275b). Third, because writing is detached from the thinker who thought what was written, it cannot speak up to explain itself; it can therefore be taken out of context, misunderstood, or misrepresented without the ability to defend itself against misinterpretation. Like paintings, writing is mute:

> written words ... [seem to speak] as if they had intelligence, but if you question them, wishing to know about their sayings, they always say only one and the same thing. And every word, when once it is written, is bandied about ... when ill-treated or unjustly reviled it always needs its father to help it; for it has no power to protect or help itself.
>
> (275d–275e)

A written text has only "words which cannot defend themselves by argument and cannot teach the truth effectually" (276c). Fourth, just as literature's representations are only imitations of appearances of things that are but imperfect copies of the true realities of the perfect forms, so writing is similarly but a copy of live oral speech which is but a copy of the real "word" of thought [*logos*] "which is written with intelligence in the mind" of the thinker (276a). Writing is a "bastard" imitation of "the living and breathing word of him who knows, of which the written word may justly be called the image" (276a).

Plato recognizes the value of literature "only for amusement" but not for the serious matters of philosophical inquiry and truth (276c). Writing's "gardens of letters [the serious thinker] ... will ... plant for amusement, and will write, when he writes, to treasure up reminders for himself, when he comes to the forgetfulness of old age," about admirable discourses on noble topics such as justice (276d). But "serious discourse about them is far nobler, when one employs the dialectic method" of living dialogue, which can make men wiser and bring men "to the farthest possible limit of human happiness" (276e–277a).

Can literature escape this critique of writing by the fact that it exists in oral forms as well? Many indeed claim that ancient Greek literature was primarily oral, more often recited and listened to than written or read.[4] Nonetheless, for an oral work to maintain its identity (through its different performances over time), it must have a reasonably defined and stable form, which could not provide the type of fully open-ended, multi-directional, dialectical give and take that Plato prizes in philosophical dialogue. A better way to resist Plato's argument against writing is to expose its performative contradiction, namely, that his rejection of doing philosophy through writing is performed through the very process of writing he rejects. Moreover, because his dialogues often involve the artistry of dramatic form, storytelling, and myth, we often appreciate his work as literature as well as philosophy.

If we understand literature broadly to include all forms of coherent, sustained, purposive, and well-wrought verbal expression, then it is hard to claim that philosophical discourse is something other than and beyond literature. It rather seems, from this perspective, that philosophy is only a distinct form of literature, one that philosophers privilege as superior to other forms. For Plato, part of that privilege is its open-ended and live dialectical character in which present thoughts are directly exchanged in real time through face-to-face dialogue. Today's new technologies enable such live dialogue in textual "chats" without face-to-face oral expression. If this means there is now less reason to privilege oral discourse over writing as being closer to thought, one could still argue that speech captures more (and more subtle) tonalities of expression than writing can. By the same logic, one could argue that remote face-to-face dialogue through internet connections such as Skype or Zoom can communicate, through facial gesture, more than a mere voice call can, while full-bodied presence allows still more forms of gestural meaning than mere oral or even face-to-face internet communication. Thus, orality itself is not the crucial, all-encompassing factor in conveying richness of meaning and truth.

Plato's *Phaedrus* suggests that philosophy can go even deeper than oral language and penetrate the realm of pure thought, that is, "the word [i.e. thought] which is written with intelligence in the mind"; the Greek word "logos" means both "word" and "thought" (Plato *Phaedrus* 276a 1925b). Can philosophy ever penetrate into a realm of truth, thought, or meaning beyond words, a realm of experience prior to and outside language? Does such a realm of raw reality or unmediated nondiscursive experience even exist? And are theorists like Maurice Blanchot right to argue, paradoxically, that only through the words of literature can we experience this nondiscursive primary reality? We address this interesting line of inquiry in Chapter 3.

Key to philosophy's claim of superiority is its commitment to truth and ennobling knowledge versus literature's alleged shallower concerns with pleasure, amusing pretense, and corruptive falsehood. If Plato defined literature not to promote its practice and understanding, but rather to diminish its importance, then, given his formative influence, subsequent philosophers, even when they eschewed Plato's condemnatory agenda, continued to define literature in inferior terms. We see this already in Aristotle's defense of literature and his recognition of imitation as the fundamental means of learning. To rescue art from the Platonic charge of mimetic preoccupation with sensuous particularities of appearance, Aristotle asserted that poetry imitates the universal and thus "is something more philosophic and of graver import than history," which treats only particular past events. This argument to defend literature only reinforces the hegemony of philosophy, because Aristotle limits poetry's cognitive value to verisimilitude – "what is possible as being probable" – rather than what is really true (Aristotle *Poetics* 1451a38–1451b10 1968).[5] Moreover, he treats literature as a distinct realm of objects set apart from ordinary life and action, sharply distinguishing the arts as *poiesis* (the making of external objects) rather than *praxis*, i.e. real action, while insisting, in his theory of catharsis, that tragedy's emotions of pity and fear are not injected into real life. Instead, they are purged in the separate realm of the theatre so that they will not affect real action or praxis (Aristotle *Nicomachean Ethics* 1140a4–10, 1140b1–25 1968; Aristotle *Poetics* 1449b21–29 1968).

Later thinkers are often far less charitable about poetry's relaxed attitude toward truth and its interest in stimulating emotions and pleasures of amusement. Francis Bacon notes how churchmen "called Poesy *Vinum Dæmonum* [devils' wine]; because it filleth the Imagination ... with the Shadow of a *Lie*," as lies "make for pleasure" (Bacon 1845: 2). Montaigne distinguishes between "telling a lie" in the sense of uttering a falsehood albeit unknowingly because one falsely believes it to be true and, on the other hand, real lying as purposefully misrepresenting things by saying "what is contrary to what [the liars] know" to be the case (Montaigne 1965: 23). On this account, writers of fiction and lyric poets employing counterfactual hyperbole would be liars, since they purposefully express things they really know are not literally true, although they may do so to amuse rather than to deceive others.

Literature as Linguistically Different and Derivative

Sir Phillip Sidney, the Renaissance poet, courtier, and soldier, offers a subtler argument against the charge that poems (and by extension, imaginative literature more generally) must lie because they involve fictional discourse. The key claim in his *An Apology for Poetry* is that literature's use of fictional discourse is altogether other than the affirming of propositions meant to be taken as true, hence the issues of truth and lying are simply not pertinent. Sidney explains that

> the poet ... nothing affirms, and therefore never lieth. For, as I take it, to lie is to affirm that to be true which is false; ... But the poet (as I said before) never affirmeth. The poet never maketh any circles about your imagination, to conjure you to believe for true what he writes. He citeth not authorities of other histories, but even for his entry calleth the sweet Muses to inspire into him a good invention; in troth, not labouring to tell you what is or is not, but what should or should not be. And therefore, though he recount things not true, yet because he telleth them not for true, he lieth not.
>
> (Sidney 1970: 57)

This strategy to free poetry and fictional literature from the calumny of lying by giving its language a special non-assertive status finds contemporary expression in analytic philosophy. Monroe Beardsley and John Searle distinguish literary language from the ordinary speech acts of assertion and other typical speech acts (such as commands, questions, promises, etc.). Instead, poetic or fictional language is only the "imitation" of such speech acts.[6] When John Donne's poem says: "Go and catch a falling star, Get with child a mandrake root," he is not really making these unreasonable commands but only imitating them. Shakespeare's "Shall I compare thee to a summer's day?" is only the imitation of a real question while his sonnet's claim "To me, fair friend, you never can be old" is not the speech act of a real assertion but only a mimetic image of such an assertion for literary purposes of expressing devoted love.

At first glance, this strategy saves literature from the calumny of lying, while distinguishing philosophy from literature. Philosophical discourse involves real speech acts in real situations involving real assertions that aim to describe the way things really are, whereas literature presents merely imitations or feigned images of real speech acts. But the matter is not so simple. Consider Plato's dialogues. Celebrated as founding paradigms of philosophy, they are not actual oral dialogues transcribed in real time, but only written representations of such dialogues as imaginatively remembered by a narrating raconteur or perhaps even invented whole cloth. In the *Symposium*, for example, the person recounting the dialogue's speeches (a certain Apollodorus) was not even present when those speeches were given but instead reports them and their dialogical context in the manner of telling a story based on someone else's eye-witness account subsequently related to him. Such narrative seems more like an imaginative representation of dialogical debate than real speech acts of dialogical assertion and questioning critique. Indeed, it closely resembles the act of storytelling that is central to the genre of literature.

Speech act theorists (like Searle) claim we can appeal to conventions and background contexts to determine whether a linguistic utterance or inscription performs a real speech act with assertive illocutionary force or only a copy thereof that is verbally identical. But there is no real-life context that precludes Plato's dialogues being read as literature rather than real philosophical assertion, especially because they are so rich in literary value. The same could be said about Montaigne's essays or those of Francis Bacon, Kierkegaard, and others. Conversely, a love poem asserting the beauty of a beloved could be written or uttered as a real assertion that honestly confesses the love that such beauty inspires in the poet.

Arthur Danto, a philosopher of art keen to preserve philosophy's scientific image, finds the idea of "philosophy-as-literature" as "something disturbing" that threatens the established idea of "philosophy-as-truth" or "philosophy as science" (Danto 1984: 151, 153, 173). He claims philosophy (like science but unlike literature) aims at universal truth. He further claims "philosophy wants to be more than universal: it wants necessity as well: truth for all the worlds that are possible," and in this it exceeds not only literature (and history) but even science which treats this world rather than all possible ones (169). It is, however, problematic to distinguish philosophy from literature by the criterion of philosophy's making true assertions about reality (let alone assertions of necessary truths for all possible worlds). This is because if truth is understood as the domain of facts about the way the world really is, then philosophical discourse, with its typically hortatory, speculative, and syntactical statements, goes well beyond the realm of factual truth.

Indeed, by the strict logical standards of Ludwig Wittgenstein's early philosophy, most philosophical statements turn out to be a form of enlightening nonsense, devoid of strict assertive meaning.[7] "It is clear," he explains in his influential *Tractatus* (1921), "that ethics cannot be put into words," and he thought the same for aesthetics and metaphysics because they transcend the world of facts and "are what is mystical" (Wittgenstein 1961: §§6.421;6.522). He claims,

> The correct method in philosophy would really be the following: to say nothing except what can be said, i.e. propositions of natural science – i.e. something that has nothing to do with philosophy – and then, whenever someone else wanted to say something metaphysical, to demonstrate to him that he had failed to give a meaning to certain signs in his propositions.
>
> (§6.54)

Wittgenstein frankly regarded his own philosophical propositions in that book as essentially "nonsensical" elucidations that simply help one to "see the world aright" but do not constitute truth or knowledge. Once the reader "has used them – as steps – to climb up beyond them. (He must, so to speak, throw away the ladder...)" (§6.54). Here philosophical writing is no different from literature in failing to make true assertions but instead showing things or inducing insights by means of language that, in strict terms of factual reference or propositional assertion, is false or meaningless. Little more than a decade later, Wittgenstein defined his general "attitude to philosophy" by claiming "philosophy ought really to be written only as a *poetic composition* [*dichten*]" (Wittgenstein 1980: 24e). Propositional truth thus fails as a compelling criterion to distinguish philosophy from literature.

A related way of linguistically distinguishing philosophy from literature is by appeal to the difference between literal language and literary language. The former is primary, serving to express literal truth about the world and constituting the essential discourse of philosophy, science, and everyday practical life. The latter is derivative and emphasizes figurative and metaphoric language designed for the expression of imaginative realms of thought. Danto affirms this essential difference. We may find "in philosophical as in scientific writing, what looks like a metaphor" but this seeming metaphor is "really ... a structural hypothesis as to how a reality we have heretofore lacked words for is to be understood" (Danto 1984: 173). What looks metaphorical is really "a fact," and the seeming metaphor acts simply as a temporary placeholder that "may be eliminated in favour of a technical term, as Locke begins ... with 'the candle within us' – and ends with the technical term *intuition*" (173).

Danto must admit that a powerful philosophical tradition rejects this hierarchical distinction of literal versus figurative language by insisting that metaphor, rather than being a derivative or irregular use of language functioning outside the realm of truth, is actually the primal form of language and the very origin of meaning and truth. Traceable to Friedrich Nietzsche, it extends into contemporaries like Derrida and Rorty who deny the radical distinction of philosophy from literature, instead affirming a view of "philosophy ... as a kind of writing" (Rorty 1982: 92).[8] Nietzsche famously argues that our notions of truth and knowledge depend on the language and concepts we use to formulate and understand them, but that such terms and concepts are the product of metaphorical identifications that are not strictly speaking true but convenient for managing our particular perceptions and experience. "Every concept originates through our equating what is unequal. No leaf ever wholly equals another, and the concept 'leaf' is formed through an arbitrary abstraction from these individual differences" by a metaphorical identification (Nietzsche 1976: 46). Hence, Nietzsche rhetorically asks (and answers):

> What, then, is truth? A mobile army of metaphors, metonyms, and anthropomorphisms – in short, a sum of human relations, which have been enhanced, transposed, and embellished poetically and rhetorically, and which after long use seem firm, canonical, and obligatory to a people. (46–7)

In short, "truths are illusions" whose original poetic, imaginative source we have forgotten, "metaphors which are worn out and without sensuous power" that have evolved into imageless concepts and truths whose figurative source has been obscured (47).[9]

If the realm of logical thought and ordinary language through which truth is formulated rests ultimately on a figurative, imaginative, poetic foundation that is primary, then imaginative literature seems superior to philosophy. We find this sort of argument, well before Nietzsche, in Percy Bysshe Shelley's *Defence of Poetry* (1840).[10] As the poetic imagination is "the principle of synthesis" that engenders and enriches language, so logic's "principle of analysis" is secondary and only deals with relations between the terms and ideas that imagination creates (Shelley 1992: 516). "For language is arbitrarily produced by the imagination," while "Reason is to imagination as the instrument to the agent" (516, 517). Shelley defines poetry as "the expression of the imagination ... [that] is connate with the origin of man" and that "creates new materials of knowledge, and power, and pleasure" (516, 526).

Moreover, instead of corrupting morals, "poetry acts to produce the moral improvement of man" through its imaginative power, while the language of "ethical science [only] arranges the elements which poetry has created" through that same imaginative power of metaphorical synthesis that "awakens and enlarges the mind itself by rendering it the receptacle of a thousand unapprehended combinations of thought" (519). Rather than the logical discourse of reason constituting the essential ground for morality, Shelley explains that

> The great secret of morals is love, or a going out of our own nature [through] ... identification of ourselves with the beautiful ... [in matters

> of others] not our own. A man, to be greatly good, must imagine intensely and comprehensively … [to] put himself in the place … of many others.
>
> (519)

Hence "The great instrument of moral good is the imagination," which poetry strengthens "in the same manner as exercise strengthens a limb" (520).

Finally, rather than belittling poetry as lacking truth and usefulness because of its focus on pleasure, Shelley insists that poetry best communicates "eternal truths" and engenders the noblest and most "durable" of pleasures that serve the most "useful" form of utility: that which "strengthens and purifies the affections, enlarges the imagination, and adds spirit to sense" (525). He concludes, "The production and assurance of pleasure in this highest sense is true utility," adding "Those who produce and preserve this pleasure are poets or poetical philosophers" (526). Totally rejecting the traditional hierarchical distinction between philosophy and poetry, Shelley affirms that true philosophers – in creating concepts, engendering new ideas, and formulating insightful truths – are really poets in the fundamental sense of being imaginative innovators through language. "Plato was essentially a poet" through "the truth and splendour of his imagery, and the melody of his language" (518). So was Lord Bacon whose language "satisfies the sense" as his "wisdom … satisfies the intellect," while "Shakespeare, Dante, and Milton (to confine ourselves to modern writers) are philosophers of the very loftiest power" in "perceiving and teaching the truth of things" (518).

Philosophy as an Embodied Way of Life

There is another way to distinguish philosophy from literature. Rather than building the distinction on differences in language, it claims that philosophy, in contrast to literature, is something more or other than language. Ancient philosophers already applied this strategy, often insisting their enterprise was a way of life rather than a form of language, that philosophy demanded expression in embodied action beyond mere utterances or textual inscriptions. Socrates is the acknowledged founder of this tradition, establishing philosophy not by producing a paradigm text or theorem but by an exemplary life, a thoughtful, dramatic model of living – and of dying. Socrates left no writings but founded philosophy by the inspiring example of his courageous quest for wisdom, which not even the threat of death could deter. Concerned with how to live a good life, this quest for wisdom recognized the need for self-knowledge through self-examination. Dedicating his life to examining his beliefs and Athenian dogma on this question of *savoir vivre*, Socrates never provided a substantive ethical code of his own. Apart from the gnomic injunctions to know and care for oneself, he left no systematic theoretical doctrines, though his disciple Plato would later formulate many through his dramatic persona.

Instead, Socrates' prime legacy was his idea and example of "the philosophical life" as a continuous, disciplined quest for the wisdom of how best to live. His actual practice of constantly seeking it embodied his answer. His life was his teaching; its practice his philosophy. If this primacy of practice makes Socrates look like a proto-pragmatist, so does his cognitive motive. The aim of self-knowledge is not truth for truth's sake, but rather ameliorative care of the self (*epimeleisthai heatou*, *ἐπιμελεῖσθαι ἑαυτοῦ*) and, as an eventual consequence, the betterment of the society in which the self is situated. In his fatal trial, Socrates claims the entire thrust of his philosophical teaching was this notion of care for the self in terms of cultivating virtue that would also benefit society as a whole. "For I go about doing nothing else than urging you, young and old, not to care for your persons or your property more than for the perfection of your souls, or even so much; and I tell you that virtue does not come from money, but from virtue comes money and all other good things to man, both to the individual and to the state"(Plato *Apology* 30a–b 1966a).[11] Rather than harming or corrupting people, Socrates claims to have "devoted [himself] to conferring upon each citizen individually what [he regarded] ... as the greatest benefit" (36c). He insists, "I tried to persuade each of you to care for himself and his own perfection in goodness and wisdom rather than for any of his belongings, and for the state itself rather than for its interests" (36c). Maintaining that the "unexamined life is not worth living," he adds in the subsequent dialogue *Crito* "that it is not living, but living well which we ought to consider most important," from which it follows that proper philosophical living is more important than writing good philosophical texts (Plato *Apology* 38a 1966a; *Crito* 48b 1966b). According to his student Xenophon, Socrates refused to "reveal [his ethical] views in a formal account" but did "so by [his] conduct," affirming the principle of *facta non verba* (Xenophon 1990: 197). "Don't you think that actions are more reliable evidence than words?" (197).

In this tradition of the philosophical life, ancient thinkers like Cicero, Epictetus, and Seneca and later Renaissance figures like Montaigne disparage as mere "grammarians," "philologist[s]," or "mathematician[s]" those philosophers who devote more "care and attention to their speech than ... to their lives," and thus "teach us how to argue instead of how to live" (Epictetus 1992: 28; Seneca 1969: 160, 207). Philosophy, in this tradition, derives her value and "authority over other arts" because she is "the mistress of the art of life itself," which is the "most valuable of all arts, the art of living well" (Montaigne 1965: 124; Seneca 1969: 171).[12] "Philosophy," says Seneca, "takes as her aim the state of happiness," not extensive book learning and prolific writing whose zealous pursuit can prove harmful (Seneca 1969: 171). Diogenes Laertius reports that Socrates was not alone among eminent ancient philosophers who "wrote nothing at all" but instead conveyed their teaching primarily through the conduct of their exemplary lives (Diogenes Laertius 1972: 16). As Montaigne writes, "To compose our character is our duty, not to compose books ... Our great and glorious masterpiece is to live appropriately" (Montaigne 1965: 850–1). Although this tradition of philosophy as a way of life has waned in modern times through the institutionalization of philosophy as an academic profession devoted to reading and writing theoretical texts, we still hear its echoes in Thoreau's famous complaint: "There are nowadays professors of philosophy, but not philosophers. Yet it is admirable to profess because it was once admirable to live" (Thoreau 1965: 14). The idea of philosophy as an art of living that extends beyond mere textual practice continues to resound in modern philosophers like Kierkegaard and Nietzsche and, in more recent times, finds advocates in philosophers with very different outlooks and methodologies: pragmatists like William James and John Dewey, poststructuralists like Michel Foucault, and scholars of ancient philosophy like Pierre Hadot. The field of somaesthetics emerged to promote this idea of philosophy as an embodied way of life that one can pursue beyond the bounds of philosophy departments and journals.[13]

William James, who originally hoped to be a painter, emphasized the importance of meanings and qualities that words cannot properly convey, and he mourned the way philosophy professors reduced the beauty and significance of those wordless values to abstract concepts and turgid verbiage. "What an awful trade that of a professor is – paid to talk, talk, talk!," James laments. "I have seen artists growing pale and sick whilst I talked to them without being able to stop. And I loved them for not being able to love me any better. It would be an awful universe if everything could be converted into words, words, words" (James 1999: 358). We find the same idea of philosophical teaching by *facta non verba* in Chinese philosophy. Confucius taught primarily by example. "We can learn from the Master's cultural refinements, but do not hear him discourse on subjects such as our natural disposition [human nature (*xing*)] and the way of *tian* [heaven (*tiandao*)]" (*Analects* 5.13; Ames and Rosemont 1998: 98). When Confucius said he "will leave off speaking" and disciples asked how he would teach them, he responded that nature teaches without speech (17.19: 208). Daoism is even more critical of language's limits. "One who knows does not speak; one who speaks does not know" (*Dao de Jing* LVI.128; Lau 1963: 63).

The idea of philosophy as an art of living involving more than words inspired the project of somaesthetics because our bodies are not merely the essential medium of life; they also provide their own forms of gestural meaning and exemplary instruction. Briefly defined, somaesthetics is the critical study and meliorative cultivation of the living, sentient, purposive body (the *soma*) as the locus of sensory appreciation (aesthesis), the formative engine of performance, and the site for creative self-fashioning. If philosophy is an art of living, then (*ceteris paribus*) we can improve our capacities in this art by cultivating the undeniably necessary medium through which this art is practiced in our world – the living, perceiving body or soma. Like the pragmatist philosophy that inspired it, somaesthetics is "a new name for some old ways of thinking," particularly the ancient idea of philosophy as an embodied way of life rather than a mere genre of theoretical discourse.[14]

There is, however, no contradiction between living and writing philosophy. The most successful ancient philosophies combined discourse and deeds, theory and practice. Even if the philosopher's actual embodied life is more important than her discourse, that life's exemplary meaning could not long survive her death without an enduring literary expression of discursive testimony. Writing provides a means of recording, communicating, and thus preserving the philosopher's model of life far beyond the immediate circle of her living presence. What would Socrates be for us without the writings of Plato and Xenophon? Indeed, philosophy established its permanence precisely through Plato's brilliantly literary account of Socrates' life and death for the sake of philosophy. Philosophical theories also typically serve as logical grounds or guiding orientations through which philosophical arts of living are developed and defended.

Epicureanism is a case in point. Holding that philosophy's prime aim was to achieve a life of happiness (conceived in terms of unmixed tranquil pleasures and best achieved through a simple, retiring life), Epicurus produced a complex theory (of human nature and the cosmos) that both justified and facilitated his art of living. Since the greatest obstacles to Epicurean happiness were anxieties caused by beliefs concerning the gods' interference in our affairs and concerning the soul's life after death, Epicurean theory tried to remove these fears by arguing that material atoms and empty space are all there is. Nature is thus governed not by divine volitions but by mere mechanical causes of atoms in space. Moreover, by claiming that even the soul is corporeal, Epicurus could argue that there is no sentience, hence no pains to fear, after the body's dissolution in death. Further, Epicurean natural theory – by indicating the nature and limits of human pains and pleasures – maintained that a pleasurable life could be attained through simple living. Thus, even if theory had "no other end in view than peace of mind," Epicurus still held it necessary for the art of living, for without theory's "study of nature there was no enjoyment of unmixed pleasures" (Diogenes Laertius 1972: 615, 667). Stoic ethics, which emphasized living in strict consistency with nature and in tranquil acceptance of its providence, likewise found support through a philosophical theory, one that viewed the whole natural world as a perfect, living organic unity, whose parts, as being necessary to the whole, must be resolutely accepted. We cannot understand Aristotle's ethical ideal of *theoria* as detached from his metaphysics that posited an unmoved mover as its divine object; and Plato's advocacy of a philosophical life devoted to seeking knowledge of the divine Forms makes little sense without a philosophical theory that showed their supreme existence and value.

My point is that there is no essential opposition compelling us to choose between philosophy as theoretical writing and as artful, embodied life-practice. Indeed, we should not choose between them. Even if we doubt that every art of living entails a full-blown philosophical theory or that every piece of philosophical writing expresses a way of life, we surely should build our art of living on our knowledge and vision of the world, and reciprocally seek the knowledge that serves our art of living. Philosophy, I believe, is strongest when both its written and more embodied modes of practice are combined to reinforce each other as they did in ancient philosophy.

Philosophy's concern with the concrete good of an individual's life does not preclude its universality or its shared social dimension. For everyone has a life to lead and the possibility to reflect on how it should be organized; and every individual life is lived in the context of others, a social and cultural background that shapes our habits, inclinations, and opinions, even when we rebel against it. Yet insofar as different individuals live in different contexts that afford or demand different possibilities of action, philosophy as a life-practice should reflect such difference. One great difference between today and ancient times is that philosophical theory no longer is a major source of knowledge of the world. The various natural and human sciences that have emerged from philosophy in modern times have assumed this function, while philosophy's role as an art of living has been largely forgotten, repressed through academic philosophy's anxious insistence on its theoretical or scientific stance.[15] Knowledge of truth is seen as the highest end and is sought for its own sake; hence "applied" philosophy is regarded as inferior. Questioning the ideal of pursuing knowledge purely for its own sake, Hellenistic philosophers like Epicurus or Seneca were more appreciative of philosophy's practical utility for enhancing virtuous practice. So was Confucius, whose goal was "to cultivate excellence" of virtue [dé 德], claiming that "Exemplary persons would feel shame if their words were better than their deeds" (*Analects* 7.3, 14.27; Ames and Rosemont 1998: 111, 178). Verbal knowledge was highly prized but largely for its instrumental value in serving crucial ends of the good life, such as virtuous behavior and self-cultivation that are not reducible to verbal formulations of truth. Montaigne similarly saw the quest for knowledge as subordinate to self-care, and he judged the ancient philosophical schools accordingly: "some sects have rather followed truth, others utility; whereby the latter have gained credit" (Montaigne 1965: 380). Pragmatism and somaesthetics represent a return to this practical, meliorative approach to philosophy as an embodied way of life.

Concerned with philosophy's use of the art of writing, this book gives particular attention to its role in philosophy as an art of living. The connection between a philosopher's life and writings can take very different forms. The favored concepts and theories of philosophers are often affirmations or justifications of the lives they have chosen and led. However, such concepts and theories can conversely serve as compensations for what they felt missing or lacking in their lives. Long before Nietzsche described philosophy as disguised autobiography (a vision of the world that justified one's life), Diogenes Laertius explained the theories of ancient Greek philosophers in terms of their life conditions and experience. The pre-Socratic Pittacus, for example, married above his social rank and then preached humility. Was this to justify the humility his wife made him practice or instead to compensate for his initial pride in taking her on? Philosophy's textual reflections of life can include inverted images. Philosophical ideals of unity and tranquility have served to compensate for lives of trouble and division but may also function as a disguised excuse for disappointed lives that secretly longed for more variety and passionate excitement. In the firm, attractive unity of a well-structured text or well-constructed theory, philosophers may be seeking the beautiful order and harmony they fail to achieve in shattered lives of tortured turmoil. As Dewey argued, philosophy's traditional quest for certainty and eternal truth represents a compensatory ideal to offset the overwhelming perils, upheavals, and uncertainties of life in ancient times.

One might read such compensatory ideals into the theories of two outstanding philosophers I have personally known and deeply admire: Richard Rorty and Jürgen Habermas. Rorty puts the concept of "conversation" at the center of his philosophical outlook, urging that "we see knowledge as a matter of conversation" and endorsing conversation rather than truth as a sufficiently worthy goal of philosophy (Rorty 1980: 171). Rejecting religion for being a "conversation-stopper," he argues:

> To see keeping a conversation going as a sufficient aim of philosophy, to see wisdom as consisting in the ability to sustain a conversation, is to see human beings as generators of new descriptions rather than beings one hopes to be able to describe accurately. To see the aim of philosophy as truth – namely, the truth about the terms which provide ultimate commensuration for all human inquiries and activities – is to see human beings as objects rather than subjects.
>
> (Rorty 1980: 378; Rorty 1999: 171)

Yet outside the lecture room, where his discourse was brilliant, Rorty was uncomfortably awkward in sustaining a conversation. One could find the same logic of conceptual compensation in the key Habermasian notions of "the ideal speech situation" and "undistorted communication" that motivate his theory of communicative action (Habermas 1970: 373; Habermas 1975: xvii). Both ideals are striking for a philosopher (born with a cleft palate) who still vocalizes his words in a manner extremely difficult to understand, despite the efforts of corrective surgery to remedy his speech distortions.

Conceived as a life-practice, philosophy is not limited to professional philosophers teaching in philosophy departments and writing for philosophical journals. Literally meaning the "love of wisdom" and defined through its Socratic paradigm, philosophy involves a critical disciplined search for wisdom that involves self-knowledge through self-examination and that aims at improving both self and society by challenging complacency and dogma.

As such, philosophy is not merely the business of a particular professional class but a project for anyone who seriously cares for her own welfare and that of society, and who is brave enough to examine herself critically and question established beliefs through a rigorous, disciplined mode of living. Socrates recommended philosophy's quest for self-knowledge and critical self-care to all members of the polis, regardless of their particular class or trade. Foucault explains how this ancient ideal of the philosophical life found renewed, albeit transformed, expression in early Christianity's forms of religious and monastic life. Here the demand for critical self-knowledge served the aim of self-cultivation as ascetic self-purification and self-sacrifice in devotion to God. To know oneself meant to know one's sins so that one could confess them and then eliminate them through rigorous disciplines of self-control aided by God's grace. Christian mystics like Saint Catherine urge us "to abide in the cell of self-knowledge" to purify ourselves in our quest for God. Providing hope for self-purification through his love and mercy, God also serves as a "mirror" of "purity" that reveals by contrast one's sins and flaws so that the soul can "better know the stains" of evil it should uproot through more arduous critical probing and discipline.[16] Such zealous commitment to uncovering all one's sins, however, can generate a morbid self-absorption that threatens the project of self-care.

Modern thinkers increasingly noted this tension between self-knowledge and self-care. Montaigne (a paradigm of self-study) claimed that honest self-examination reveals "an object that fills us with discontent; we see nothing in us but misery and vanity. In order not to dishearten us, Nature has very appropriately thrown the action of our vision outward" (Montaigne 1965: 766). Likewise, although Immanuel Kant affirms that "the First Command of all Duties to Oneself … is 'know (scrutinize, fathom) yourself,'" he nonetheless warns that this involves a "descent into the hell of self-cognition" even if such descent is necessary to "pave the way to godliness" (Kant 1996: 191). This hell of self-cognition, the self-destructive danger of prying into dark secrets of the self, is key to the tragedy of Oedipus, where the loving Jocasta (his mother and wife) warns him "pray you don't discover who you are!' (Sophocles 2011: 66). Steeped in Greek tragedy, Nietzsche similarly cautions that introspective "digging into one's self, this straight, violent descent into the pit of one's being, is a painful and dangerous undertaking" (Nietzsche 1999a: 340). Nietzsche thus gives preference to the creative, dynamic project of self-transformation, "to become what one is"; a project for which "*nosce te ipsum* [know yourself] would be the recipe for destruction" (Nietzsche 1992: 34). Goethe similarly condemns the zeal for self-examination as "a device of secretly bound priests" that brings "psychological torments" and unhealthily directs us "away from the activities of the outer world to an inner false contemplation" (Goethe 1966: 479; Goethe 1955: 38). Instead, he argues, one can know oneself better by knowing one's world, which includes knowing one's place in it among other things and other persons. By comparing our views of life with others, we can achieve a more objective and nuanced self-knowledge than we could acquire through introspection. In short, a one-sided diet of introspection is not only psychologically damaging, it is epistemologically inadequate for self-knowledge and self-cultivation.

To know the self more fully we need to represent it in some way so that both we and others can better examine it. The art of writing can play a crucial role here in presenting representations of the self that are not only durable (*littera scripta manet*) but eminently shareable. Recording the self through attractive writing will reward the attention of others (including one's own future self) and thus enable new insights and perspectives. Though it may weaken the powers of spontaneous memory, the art of writing extends our capacity to remember by providing enduring reminders. Philosophy as an art of living is not concerned with memories simply for their own sake but rather for how they help to understand the self in order to improve it. Presenting one's views, oneself, in writing enables repeated critical assessment that can inspire and guide one's efforts of meliorative self-transformation.

Though most ancient philosophical traditions identified the self with an enduring immortal soul, modern thinking typically regards the self as a dynamic product continuously in the making. Explicitly building on Nietzsche and recognizing that self-care can override self-knowledge, Foucault urges that writing about the self should focus more on self-transformation than self-analysis, seeking to escape or transcend (rather than report or dwell on) the limits of the self's present state. If "the main interest in life and work is to become someone else that you were not in the beginning," then the practice of writing provides an excellent way both to transform oneself and to hide one's self behind a faceless maze of words (Foucault 1988: 9). "I am no doubt not the only one who writes in order to have no face," claims Foucault. "Do not ask who I am and do not ask me to remain the same" (Foucault 1972: 17). By creating a textual persona to disguise and protect the self from direct, physical exposure to the public (which could prove inhibiting and risky), one has greater liberty for imaginative experiments that challenge the limits of the self and the social conventions that define those limits. Texts exist as real things in the world while creating worlds of their own. Writing provides an imaginative realm in the real world for bold explorations of possible selves that one can fictionally assume and critically assess, while carefully guarding one's real or ideal self apart. In adopting this strategy of exploration and concealment, Kierkegaard deployed a host of pseudonyms.

Notwithstanding its benefits in shielding or hiding the self behind veils of textual constructions, fictions, and even pseudonyms, literature is crucially beneficial for transforming the self through public exposure. Literary composition rescues the self from the privacy of one's thoughts, feelings, and imaginative efforts of self-knowledge and self-care. The created textual persona can significantly reshape the author's own lived self and subjectivity, impelling her to bring her actual, personal self to conform more closely to her textual identity. I deliberately use the feminine pronoun here because two of the twentieth century's most important female philosophers (Hannah Arendt and Simone de Beauvoir) insist on the value of literature for liberating woman's project of self-realization from the oppressively stifling confinement of self-examining introspection, of private, ephemeral interiority.

Arendt's book on Rahel Varnhagen (née Levin), the turn-of-the-nineteenth-century Jewish salon intellectual, stresses the importance of Rahel's literary practice of letter writing as necessary for her self-realization by ensuring that her rich inner life found external expression in a literary form that made her thoughts no longer ephemeral and private. In the same way, her reading of literature (especially Goethe) gave her the tools not only to experience life more subtly but also to capture and convey that experience in precise and preserving language. "The function of language is preservation" and what literature embodies can "remain longer than is possible for ephemeral human beings" (Arendt 1997: 170–1). Through her absorption in literature's "absolute precision in the use of words," "Rahel acquired to the point of mastery the art of representing her own life" to others and thus emerging more confidently beyond her inner world into the real "intricacies of social life" (171, 173). "She had learned that the pure subjectivity which makes a point of 'bearing a world within itself' is doomed because this inner world" rests too narrowly on the mere contingency of the individual's experience without sufficient support by broader social existence and recognition (173). Through literary writing, even in the form of letters that she circulated among her friends, social recognition of one's distinctive personhood could be achieved; and through such recognitional processes the self could be transformed.

In *The Second Sex*, Simone de Beauvoir continuously cautions against the special dangers that introspective self-examination poses for women. Distanced from the life of public action and essentially confined to the private domain of caring for home, husband, and children, woman is already overly inclined to "being occupied with herself" in the realm of contemplative interiority, "to study her sensations and unravel their meaning" (Beauvoir 1989: 623, 626). Relegated to the essential role of ornament whose value depends on always presenting a charming appearance, woman is already too absorbed in critical self-analysis of what she is and how she looks to achieve a radical transformation of her condition in the world. "She still regards her life as an immanent enterprise," measured by "subjective success" (702). Rather than self-analysis, "what woman essentially lacks today for doing great things is forgetfulness of herself," an escape from critical subjective immanence so that she can project herself boldly and forcefully into the world of action and transcendence (702). Given the societal conventions that constrained the possibilities of women to make a public mark in the world, writing represented for Beauvoir an extremely important mode of transcendence and public recognition. Beauvoir always proudly defined herself as a writer more than a philosopher. If this served to distinguish herself from her lifelong lover and collaborator Jean-Paul

Sartre (who proudly donned the philosopher's crown), it also underlined the fact that her strictly philosophical texts are few compared to her output in other genres, such as novels, travel and political essays, and memoirs. Beauvoir's extensive autobiographical writings demonstrate that she viewed the art of writing as an indispensable tool for converting self-analysis into active transcendence in the public sphere. "This was the meaning behind my vocation," she writes in examining her early years, "I would take my own childhood in hand again and make of it a faultless work of art. I saw myself as the basis of my own apotheosis" (Beauvoir 1959: 57). Transcribing one's feelings and thoughts in a literary form can transform the self not only by going beyond its interior experience but also by reshaping the self in a more compelling narrative that supports further activity of transformational transcendence.

If these twentieth-century feminist thinkers highlighted writing for the philosophical life of meliorative self-transformation that transcends the private self to transform society, modern times have witnessed other models of the philosophical life. Foucault presents the nineteenth-century political revolutionary as one example, someone who lived a radically risky life of combative divergence to destroy established beliefs and institutions and replace them with higher truths and ideals. The modern artist's distinctively unconventional style of living and self-sacrificing devotion to art is another version of the philosophical life that bears witness to the form of truth it embodies (here the truth of art) by its difference from common ways of living. The idea, as Foucault puts it, is "that the artist's life, in the very form it takes, should constitute some kind of testimony of what art is in its truth. The artist's life must not only be sufficiently singular for him to be able to create his work, but it must in some way be a manifestation of art itself in its truth," the truth that "art is capable of giving a form to existence which breaks with every other form, a form which is that of the true life" (Foucault 2011: 187).[17]

This provides further reason to soften the literature/philosophy distinction. We should not exclude literary artists from the field of philosophy. Not only do their texts distinctively express important philosophical ideas, but they surely can practice the philosophical life in its artistic form – living a life that not only generates their literary creation but also bears embodied witness to the truth their texts express. In studying how writing serves and shapes the philosophical life, this book considers both philosophical and literary authors, while focusing especially on writers who straddle the presumed philosophy/literature divide.

Notes

1 For my citations from Plato's *Republic* and his other dialogues, I generally use the translations found in H.N. Fowler, W.R.M. Lamb, R.G. Bury, and Paul Shorey (eds.), *Plato in Twelve Volumes* (Cambridge, MA: Harvard University Press, initially published in 1925, and available digitally at http://www.perseus.

tufts.edu. I cite in parenthesis the Stephanus numbers through which one refers to Plato's works in their different translations and published editions, and then give the year of the edition I am using. Occasionally, I prefer the translations found in John M. Cooper and D.S. Hutchinson (eds.), *Plato: Complete Works* (Indianapolis: Hackett Publishing Company, 1997). Those citations will also include the page number from that 1997 Hackett edition.

2 See the classic study of K.J. Dover, *Greek Homosexuality* (Cambridge, MA: Harvard University Press, 1978), 94–103. For a broader account of the role of sexuality in ancient philosophy, not only Greco-Roman theory but also Christian, Chinese, Indian, Islamic, and Japanese thought, see Richard Shusterman, *Ars Erotica: Sex and Somaesthetics in the Classical Arts of Love* (Cambridge: Cambridge University Press, 2021).

3 Plato displays an ambivalent attitude toward divine possession and the female gender, because his hero Socrates famously had a demon that hauntingly guided him by warning him what paths of thought and action not to take, and Socrates also claimed to learn some of his loftiest ideas from the female priestess Diotima.

4 Pierre Hadot insists that "the written works of this [ancient] period remain closely tied to oral conduct" and "were intended to be read aloud, ... since in antiquity reading customarily meant reading aloud, emphasizing the rhythm of the phrase and the sound of the words." Orality, he argues, was also important for written philosophy of that time because the texts of philosophers generally served as "a preparation, extension, or echo of their spoken lessons." Pierre Hadot, *Philosophy as a Way of Life*, trans. Michael Chase (Oxford: Blackwell, 1995), 62.

5 My citations from Aristotle refer to the Bekker numbers and the translation in Richard McKeon (ed.), *The Basic Works of Aristotle* (New York: Random House, 1968).

6 Monroe Beardsley, *The Possibility of Criticism* (Detroit: Wayne State University Press, 1970); John Searle, "The Logical Status of Fictional Discourse," *New Literary History*, 6:2 (1975), 319–32.

7 Ludwig Wittgenstein, *Tractatus Logico-Philosophicus*, trans. D.F. Pears and B.F. McGuinness (London: Routledge, 1961). I refer parenthetically to the book's passage numbers rather than pages, and my final quote from Wittgenstein in this paragraph is from an entry in his secret notebooks, published in German and English in G.H. Von Wright (ed.), *Culture and Value* (Oxford: Blackwell, 1980), 24; I use my translation.

8 Stanley Cavell, a philosopher whose extensive work on interpreting Shakespeare spans the philosophy/literature divide, knows that their relation remains "contentious." "Some say that philosophy is literature, some say it is science, some say it is ideology," while Cavell suggests it is deeply related to autobiography and the claim of a person as philosopher "to speak for the human" in general. Stanley Cavell, *A Pitch of Philosophy* (Cambridge MA: Harvard University Press, 1994), vii.

9 The argument and quotes here come from a posthumously published fragment written in 1873, whose partial English translation appears in Walter Kauffman (ed.), *The Portable Nietzsche* (New York: Vintage, 1954), 47.

10 My references to this text are from its version in Hazard Adams (ed.), *Critical Theory Since Plato* (New York: Harcourt, Brace, Javonovich, 1992), 515–29.

11 This notion of *epimeleisthai* in terms of "to care for" is sometimes translated as "taking pains with" or "cultivation."

12 In Greek, Latin, and French (as well as other languages), the word for philosophy is a grammatically female gendered noun.

13 See Richard Shusterman, *Practicing Philosophy: Pragmatism and the Philosophical Life* (London: Routledge, 1997); *Body Consciousness: A Philosophy of Mindfulness and Somaesthetics* (Cambridge: Cambridge University

Press, 2008); *Thinking through the Body: Essays in Somaesthetics* (Cambridge: Cambridge University Press, 2012).

14 William James, *Pragmatism: A New Name for Some Old Ways of Thinking* (New York: Longmans, 1907); I adopt James's words to characterize the project of somaesthetics in my books *Pragmatist Aesthetics* (2000); *Body Consciousness* (2008), and *Thinking through the Body* (2012).

15 The philosophical impact of modern science is only one reason for the decline of the idea of philosophy as a special way of life. An earlier and complementary reason was Christianity's absorption of the philosophical life's ideals of spiritual *askesis* and self-improvement, coupled with medieval Scholasticism's subordination of philosophy to theology, where philosophy served as merely a conceptual, theoretical tool for the latter. As Hadot describes this process: "Theology became conscious of its autonomy *qua* supreme science, while philosophy was emptied of its spiritual exercises, which, from now on, were relegated to Christian mysticism and ethics. Reduced to the rank of a 'handmaid of theology,' philosophy's role was henceforth to furnish theology with conceptual – and hence purely theoretical – material. When, in the modern age, philosophy regained its autonomy, it still retained many features inherited from this medieval conception. In particular, it maintained its purely theoretical character" (Hadot 1995: 107–8).

16 St. Catherine, "A Treatise of Discretion," in *The Dialogue of St. Catherine*, trans. Algar Thorold (New York: Cosimo Classics, 1907), 62.

17 Foucault's particular focus in this lecture is on the philosophical life of the Cynics.

2 Writing, Identity, and the Unity of Self

The Art of Living and the Value of Unity

Philosophy is not a monolithic field. It has different conceptions of what constitutes wisdom, and includes philosophers with very different ideas, personalities, and living conditions, so we find diverse forms of its art of living. Although Socrates established the formative model of the philosophical life, he never defined it precise terms, and ancient philosophers understood it in various ways. Apart from the notions of wisdom and virtue (and partly to explain them), Plato proposes two different models of philosophical care for the self that were influential throughout antiquity, a quasi-medical one of health through therapy and an aesthetic model of art and beauty.[1] In dialogues such as *Crito*, *Gorgias*, and *Republic*, he suggests the philosopher's role is analogous to the physician's. As the latter cares for the body's health, the philosopher aims at improving the soul's. But philosophy is superior to medicine, since the physician's quest is doomed, in the end, to failure. For while the body's health must be ultimately undermined by death, the immortal soul's is not so limited. The aesthetic model of philosophical life, compellingly portrayed in Plato's *Symposium* (204c–212b), defines love's desire for beauty as the source of philosophy and describes the philosophical life of self-care as a continuous quest for ever higher forms of beauty that ennobles the philosopher. This quest is not simply to enjoy "beautiful things" (ranging from bodily beauty to "the beauty of activities and laws" to the ideal form of "the Beautiful itself") but also "to beget" or "give birth" to the beautiful: "beautiful ideas and theories," "beautiful deeds," and the beauty of "true virtue" (Plato *Symposium* 209b–212b 1997: 491–4). These beautiful creations, like the begetting of children, derive from life's drive for immortality, and they help us achieve it by remaining after one's death as beautiful memorials of one's life. This life of beauty, Socrates concludes, is what wins the philosopher "the love of the gods" so that "if any human being could become immortal, it would be he" (212a–212b: 494). Given such an aesthetic model of philosophy, Socrates and Plato were

DOI: 10.4324/9780429331770-2

understandably keen to emphasize art's inferiority and its risks for the beautiful conduct of life.

Key to the ideals of health and beauty were the values of unity and order, which indeed were essential values for virtually all ancient theories of philosophical life as self-knowledge and self-care. Whether life's highest goal was pleasure, knowledge, or virtue through wisely rational control, philosophers advocated unity and order, since disorder brought conflict, confusion, turmoil, dissipation, and loss of control. For the beauty-loving Greeks, a good life was a beautiful life; and unity was perceived as essential not only to beauty and good order, but even to existence or being itself. As Plotinus remarks, "It is in virtue of unity that beings are beings," and he argued that beauty is loved because it best exemplifies the unity of being (Plotinus 1991: 535). "Beauty without Being could not be, nor Being voided of Beauty: abandoned by Beauty, Being loses something of its essence. Being is desirable because it is identical with Beauty; and Beauty is loved because it is Being. How then can we debate which is the cause of the other, where the nature is one?" (420). "We ourselves possess beauty when we are true to our own being; our ugliness is in going over to another order; our self-knowledge, that is to say, is our beauty; in self-ignorance we are ugly" (424).

Philosophers have offered various, sometimes overlapping strategies for attaining the necessary unity: reason, moderation, ascetic self-control, and withdrawal from the complexities of politics, marriage, and children. One leading strategy was the positing of a clear, unifying hierarchy of powers or values (such as reason over desire, soul over body, knowledge over pleasure). Another was the unifying singularity of what Epictetus called a ruling principle. "You must be one person ... You must either work on your ruling principle or work on externals, practice the art either of what is inside or of what is outside, that is, play the role of the philosopher or of a non-philosopher" (Epictetus 1992: 20). As the Roman Stoic philosopher (and emperor) Marcus Aurelius explains, "If a man's life has no consistent and uniform aim it cannot itself remain consistent or uniform," and it should conform to his "true self" for the man to "achieve consistency with himself" (Marcus Aurelius 1964: 175, 176).

This chapter examines how writing serves the quest to find unity in oneself to promote philosophy's aims of self-knowledge and self-care. We focus on four influential authors from different epochs and linguistic cultures, who straddle the fields of literature and philosophy: Augustine, Montaigne, Wordsworth, and Kierkegaard. Study of these authors reveals how writing not only provides promising strategies for achieving self-unity but also evokes feelings of inconsistency, fragmentation, or alienation. That writing, even in the philosophical quest for unity and knowledge, paradoxically leads to disunity and doubt (through the slippery nature of language and the alterity of the text) is an idea that vividly recalls the ancient quarrel and enduring tension between philosophy and literature.

Augustine

Saint Augustine (354–430) was born to a Catholic mother and pagan father in the North African part of the Roman Empire. Shaped by the ancient tradition of Greco-Roman philosophy and early Christianity (which became the official religion of the Roman Empire in 323), Augustine made the art of Latin writing and rhetoric the foundational springboard and sustaining engine of his entire career. His early education "was frankly pagan" and "exclusively literary," focusing on "eloquence acquired" through rigorous training in classics of Latin literature, such as Virgil and Cicero (Brown 2000: 24; Augustine *Confessions* I.XVI: 1993: 15).[2] Already as a schoolboy, he developed a passion for "stage shows" and even won a prize for his oral rendition of a dramatic text expressing the goddess Juno's grief and rage (I.XVI, I.XIX: 16, 18). This love of theatre and its romantic passions grew even stronger when he moved to Carthage ("a cauldron of illicit loves") to study and later teach "the art of Rhetoric" (III.I, IV.II: 35, 51). By "studying the books of eloquence; for in eloquence it was [his] ambition to shine," he eventually won "a contest for a poem to be recited on stage" that led (in 383) to a job of teaching rhetoric in Rome (III.IV, IV.II: 38, 52).

By that time Augustine had taken a concubine (with whom he fathered a son) and had published a book of literary theory (no longer extant) on the beautiful and fitting. He also had extended his studies to Manichean theology and Greek philosophy. Once in Rome, he won the superior appointment of "professor of Rhetoric" in Milan on the strength of "a public oration" (V.XIII: 81–2). As Milan was then the capital of the Western Roman Empire, the professor's job involved composing "official panegyrics on the Emperor" and texts describing "programmes of the court," so Augustine's move to Milan put him near the highest circles (Brown 2000: 58–9). This included proximity to Saint Ambrose, a distinguished theologian and Milan's archbishop, who was deeply admired not only by Augustine but also, most zealously, by his mother who had come to join Augustine in Milan and compelled him to abandon his concubine and to acquire a well-connected local fiancée who was too young to marry immediately. Augustine, however, never married because he grew increasingly attracted to the ideal of Christian celibate life; yet he struggled to master his sexual desire, briefly taking another concubine and famously praying: "Grant me chastity and continence, but not yet" (VIII.VII: 139).

What ultimately convinced him to be chaste and to convert officially to the Catholic faith was a mystical experience in which he heard a mysterious child-like voice repeatedly chanting in "a sort of sing-song" the words "Take and read, take and read" (VIII.XII: 146). This prompted Augustine to take his book of scriptures, which magically opened to a Pauline verse urging service to Christ by shedding all concupiscence. It is significant that rather than being inspired by a divine visual image, Augustine's conversion derived from the hearing of words and the reading of literature. Deciding to resign his post in rhetoric and no longer "sell the art of words," he never abandoned this art but instead put all his talent for "writing ... now in [God's] service" (IX.IV, IX.V: 154, 157). Even after returning to North Africa, where he was extremely busy with practical matters as a priest and then Bishop of Hippo, Augustine was writing all the time, ultimately producing a corpus of still existing texts that numbers more than five million words.

Fresh from his conversion in 386, he quickly composed a series of four books that sought to integrate Platonic philosophy with Christian thought in tackling the classical question of the art of living and the ideal life "in Philosophy" (Brown 2000: 109). The books are *Contra Academicos*, *De Beata Vita*, *De Ordine*, and *Soliloquia* (Brown 2000: 110–11). The first three are dialogues with characters from Augustine's most intimate circle of friends and family, while *Soliloquia* is a soul-searching internal dialogue between himself and reason, and is similarly concerned with the key philosophical task of "inquiring both concerning [oneself] and [one's] chief good" (Augustine *Soliloquies* 1.1.1: 1888: 537).

The question of literature plays an important role in these discussions, as Augustine strives to reconcile the old Platonic quarrel between philosophy (his newer love) and literature (the beloved art that brought him success and led him to philosophy, and eventually to God). He argues that although "philosophy is more beautiful" and should "claim for herself a greater share of [one's] affection than the discipline of poetry," the writing of "poets shouldn't be completely disregarded by philosophy," because poetry shares with philosophy the profound "care about order" (Foley 2015: 20, 22; translated from Augustine *Contra Academicos* 3.1.1, 3.6.13; cf. 1948a: 168, 182; Augustine *De Ordine* 1.8.21: 1948b: 259). It also shares the values and mastery of unity, "right reasoning and ... the power of numbers" through its essential concern with regulating meter, structure, and harmony (Augustine *De Ordine* 2.18.47: 1948b: 324). Although rejected as a final end in itself, Augustine affirms poetry as extremely useful for leading us to philosophy and truth. This is because it teaches us to enjoy and love the ordered beauty of truth yet cannot (through its pagan fictions and sensual, this-worldly concerns and pleasures) properly satisfy that love, so that we more "ardently seek and more consistently pursue and in the end more lovingly cling to [that higher truth of divine philosophy that makes] the happy life" (Augustine *De Ordine* 1.8.24: 1948b: 261).

Another work begun shortly thereafter, *De Musica*, likewise urged using the arts to lead us from the order of beauty and truth in material things to appreciating its source in the perceiving soul and ultimately in God. Not devoted to music per se, the book studies the poetic principles of meter and then evolves into a metaphysics of order. It conceives music as "the science of mensurating [measuring] well" and regards number as the key principle of measure and order that regulates the universe, with God being the creative source of that principle as being the most perfect unity and number, the *One* (Augustine *De*

Musica 1.2.2, 6.7.17: 1947: 172, 341–2).[3] The quest for self-knowledge and self-care through perception of "the order of reality" and its divine source "by which this world is truly held together and governed" defines Augustine's early conception of the philosophical life (Augustine *De Ordine* 1.1.1: 1948b: 239).

> To philosophy pertains a twofold question: the first treats of the soul; the second, of God. The first makes us know ourselves; the second our origin. The former is the more delightful to us; the latter, more precious. The former makes us fit for a happy life; the latter renders us happy. The first is for beginners; the latter, for the well instructed. This is the order of wisdom's branches of study by which one becomes competent to grasp the order of things.
>
> (Augustine *De Ordine* 2.18.47: 1948b: 324)

Augustine came to realize that this step-by-step methodology was mistakenly naïve and overconfident. A decade later, when writing his *Confessions*, already as an experienced bishop and approaching middle age, he found those earlier works too rich with pagan poetry and "still smacked of the school of pride" (Augustine *Confessions* IX.IV: 1993: 154). Augustine now argues that the human mind is too weak and obscure for proper self-knowledge and self-care; it is too sinfully volatile and muddled to establish a stable, healthy unity and order in one's being. Poignantly "terrified by [his] sins and the mass of [his] misery," he saw the need to seek and gain the grace of God to guide this quest, because God knows us better than we know ourselves, and it is only *through* and *in* God that we can find the saving truth and a stable, satisfying unity of being (X.XLIII: 208). A trailblazing literary work of art, *Confessions* is also a writerly philosophical exercise in personal, soul-searching meditation, an extended process of therapy aimed at better knowledge and care of the self through the self-order and unity achieved through the wholehearted love of God. Its restorative cure is fascinating not only because the writing is so beautiful but also because its project of healing unity and truth embraces so many rich ambiguities and paradoxical tensions.

We can study its philosophical argument by analyzing those tensions, beginning with its very title, deriving from the Latin "*confessio*" (originally from the biblical Hebrew *yadah* יָדָה) whose contrasting meanings produce polysemic richness. The term (in either language) has both the negative sense of acknowledging a wrongdoing or sin and the positive meaning of thanking or praising. In confessing to God, one not only regretfully avows misdoings but also praises and thanks God for the greatness of his works and the blessings one enjoys while implicitly praying that such thanks and praise and penitent admission of sins will manifest one's love of God and ensure God's continuing mercy and forgiveness. Hence, Augustine's *Confessions* is not so much a chastened memoir of transgression as an uplifting hymn of praise and thanks to his God.

Having earlier led a wayward life, wandering both geographically and intellectually, Augustine sought a secure harbor of self-identity to provide the needed focus for self-knowledge and self-care. Paradoxically, to find that stable unity in himself, he must find it through God's love, as "our hearts are restless till they rest in Thee" (Augustine *Confessions* I.I: 1993: 3). His confession of "past wickedness" and chaotic "carnal corruptions" serves to magnify his love of God's "Loveliness" and healing oneness (II.I: 23). "I collect my self out of that broken state in which my very being was torn asunder because I was turned away from Thee, the One, and wasted myself upon the many," writes Augustine (II.I: 23). In order "to return to myself," he continues, "I entered my own depths with You as guide and ... helper" (VII.X: 117–18). Another reason why self-knowledge requires God's help and love is that God knows us better than we can ever know ourselves, because to God's "eyes the deepest depth of man's conscience lies bare" (X.II: 173). "What I know of myself I know through the shining of Your light; and what I do not know of myself, I continue not to know until my darkness shall be made as noonday in Your countenance" (X.V: 176). As we gain God's insightful love by loving God, so we best love God by seeking to know him.

If this suggests that proper self-knowledge and self-care require shifting the focus from self to God, then Augustine again reverses the focus by arguing that we can best know and love God by returning to ourselves through a confession that shows our striving for such knowledge and love. We praise God's perfection, beauty, and merciful goodness in contrast to our sins and ugliness while also appreciating the way he pardons our evils and enlightens our ignorance. "Let me know Thee, who knowest me, let me know Thee, even as I am known ... For behold Thou lovest the truth, and he that does the truth comes to the light" (X.I: 173). Augustine hopes to come into the light of knowledge by "doing" the truth, and the way he seeks to do the truth in loving God is precisely by *confession*. "I wish to do it in confession, in my heart before Thee, in my writing before many witnesses" as this will show "I delight in You and love You and ... am ashamed of what I am" (X.II: 173).

Although autobiographical, *Confessions* neglects many important details of Augustine's life; we never even learn the name of his concubine of 15 years or that of the close young friend whose early death almost drove him to despair. Augustine concentrates instead on the feelings and thoughts that arose in his mind from his interaction with people, events, and ideas. Less a memoir than a psychological study, this retrospective narrative is also, Augustine insists, not concerned with describing who he was but rather in revealing who he now is, as he girds himself to lead a better Christian life but also to lead his flock as a bishop and renowned theologian. "I confess unto men ... in this book, not what I once was, but what I now am" (X.III: 174). To emphasize the point, he repeats it, highlighting his conflicting feelings (exultation and sorrow) and contrasted target audiences (human and divine). It is "the confession not of what I have been, but of what I am—in that I confess not only before You, with inward exultation yet trembling, with inward sorrow yet with hope as well: but also in the ears of the believing sons of men, companions of my joy and sharers of my mortality, my fellow citizens, fellow pilgrims," who unlike God, "have not their ear at my heart, where I am what I am" (X.III–IV: 174–5). Many of these "desire to know" God's mercy toward Augustine and could profit from such knowledge, but require Augustine's writing to reveal it (X.III: 174). For those many "You command me to serve I will show, not what I was, but what I now am, what I continue to be" (X.IV: 175). It is evident that Augustine is writing from his present, devoutly Catholic state of mind and that he describes his past deeds, feelings, and beliefs as largely sinful, and describes them very differently from the ways he must have experienced them in his past. But it is equally true that this past experience helped constitute who he presently is, as it indeed led him, albeit somewhat circuitously, to his current status and state of mind. Self-knowledge might seem easier if we could dismiss the past, because, as Augustine laments, our memory of the past is painfully weak and fallible. Moreover, its difference from the present self (which is particularly acute in cases of conversion) raises the problem of self-unity or identity that seems essential to self-knowledge and self-care. Yet what would self-knowledge be without the knowledge of the self's past?

Autobiography provides a remedy for this multiplication of the self because it integrates past and present, and even future-looking thoughts. The unity of narrative provides an aesthetic unification to compensate for the loss of psychological and cognitive unity due to the fading of memory and the disruption of attitudes through personal transformation. In a finely wrought written narrative, one can put oneself all together again in a compelling, attractive order. The remedy of writing, however, involves a different doubling of self. There is the subject-self or "I" who writes, but there is also the object-self or "Me" that the "I" describes in writing (whether in the past, present, or future). Moreover, even the subject-self suffers duplication, because besides the "I" who writes, there is also the "I" who reads and reacts to the writing. Although writing can fix a single, permanent order of words, the reading subject's consciousness continues to change with time and may read the same words in different ways. Augustine makes his role as reader central to his writing of *Confessions*, which seeks to inspire by its verbal beauty and thus fortify his faith and intensify his energy for further holy work of service.

> When the confession of my past sins—which You have forgiven and covered up, giving me joy in You, changing my life by faith and Your sacrament—are read and heard, they stir up the heart. It no longer lies in a lethargy of despair and says "I cannot."
>
> (X.III: 174)

He later confirms this reader-oriented motive of writing. These confessions to God are not for God's own already omniscient knowledge, "but [to] excite my own love for You and the love of those who read what I write" (XI.I: 211). Thus, this text to unify the self is also not united in its target of readership.

If Augustine rejoices in the empowering beauty of his literary art, he avoids sinful pride by recognizing not only that this beauty has its true source in the all-beautiful God who inspires his thought and language, but also that the beauty of his words, like all human language, is nothing compared to the supreme beauty of God's creation. Augustine is deeply aware of the complexities and tensions of writing. His words are his, yet inspired by and directed to God. The many quotations from scriptures that he weaves into his personal, literary text are divine words delivered through God's prophets and apostles, if not directly by God. Yet Augustine, through writing, makes these words his own. An amalgam of worldly and otherworldly words, his text can serve as a general emblem for the complex ontology of the literary work, which exists in the material world but also constitutes a world of its own. Moreover, as God gave his scriptures in Hebrew and Greek, not in Latin, Augustine's own original text already involves the complexities of translation, betraying inherent multiplicity rather than oneness.

Augustine is extremely sensitive to the equivocal, fallen nature of human words and the complexities, ambiguities, and risks of writing; the painful gap between the language of humans and the Word of God pervades *Confessions*. Belonging to the temporal, material world, human words suffer the limits and alterations of time. A text's words may remain unchanged through the passage of time, but this cannot ensure it having a single, permanent true meaning; new interpretations arise as words acquire new meanings. Textual corruptions arise through errors, and some texts may be irretrievably lost, as was Augustine's own book on the beautiful and fitting. In contrast, God's "Word was incorruptible, because it was ... one and the same substance" with God, and Augustine cites scripture "that in the beginning was the Word and the Word was with God and the Word was God" (VII.II, VII.IX: 109, 116). In contrast to the temporal limits of "our own tongue, in which a word has both beginning and ending," the divine "Word ... abides in Himself forever, yet grows not old and makes all things new" (IX.X: 164). The "poverty of the human intellect [compensates with] an abundance of words" that cover their emptiness with fine noise (XII.I: 235). God's Word instead is silent but all powerful and "co-eternal with [Himself]," claims Augustine: "in one eternal act You say all that You say, and all things are made that You say are to be made" (XI.VII: 215).

What Augustine finds most troubling in language and literature is not their limits of efficacy and their temporal, mutable, imperfect nature, but rather their ambivalent power for abuse as well as benefit. The art of words can inspire vice rather than virtue, can deceive and corrupt with lies rather than enlighten and redeem with truth. Augustine laments that his early education in eloquence was acquired through the "vileness" of lustful tales of classic pagan literature. He admits "the words ... in themselves are choice and precious vessels," but they carry "the wine of error" that makes one drunk with the illicit lusts they describe, and he "sinfully delighted in them" (I.XVI: 16). Still worse than literature's lustful fictions were the lies of false philosophies, as the former were "less harmful" because less believed, whereas Augustine once believed the Manichean philosophers he now condemns as "talking high-sounding nonsense, carnal and wordy men" (III.VI: 39–40). Rather than truth, that false Manichean philosophy "was all words—words spoken, words written in many huge tomes" (III.VI: 39). Its philosophers used the best and holiest of words "but only as sounds and tongue noises; for their heart was empty of the true meaning" (III.VI: 39).

Sensitive to the beauty of song and the resonant rhythm of verse, and worried that this love of sound was a sinful attachment to sensuous pleasure, Augustine was also wary of the power of speech to bewitch its hearers and to disturb the purity of silent, spiritual meditation on God and holy things. He makes his confession in writing to secure this noiseless communication, that is paradoxically both silent and not, because it speaks his heart with only "the voice of [his] pen" (XI.II: 211). "And so my confession ... is made silently: and yet not silently, for if it makes no sound, yet it cries aloud in my heart," and resounds in the written words that resonate with readers (X.II: 173). Writing's power of soundless spiritual communication suggests that contrary to Plato's view in *Phaedrus*, voiced speech may be farther from the pure *logos* of thought than writing is.

As God is the source and guarantee of truth, so the art of devotional writing constitutes a key instrument for acquiring new knowledge. Not surprisingly, Augustine's next book, on the Trinity, makes a stark avowal of writing's power for cognitive discovery as well as communication. "I must confess that, personally, I have learned many things I never knew before ... just by writing" (Brown 2000: 270). He confesses the point again in a letter written in 412, while preparing his magnum opus the *City of God*: "I am the sort of man who writes because he has made progress, and who makes progress—by writing" (354). In that same letter, however, Augustine recognizes that his progress remains partial and his writings all too fallible and needing correction. "If God permit me, I shall gather together and point out, in a work specially devoted to this purpose, all the things which justly displease me in my books" (354). He worked long and hard on that self-critical project that focused on his major books and was published as *Retractiones* in 427, although he continued to write and publish until his death in 430. Noting with apprehension the warning of Proverbs 10:19 that "In the multitude of words, sin is not lacking," Augustine admits, "I am afraid ... that, from my works, which are so many, it would be possible to collect much, which, if not false, would seem to be, or revealed to be unnecessary" (Brown 2000: 433, citing *Retractiones*, Prol.,1). He did not renounce, however, the impassioned poetry of his *Confessions*, which taught him by bringing him closer to God's love and thus nearer to unifying, knowing, and caring for himself as God's devoted, lifelong servant.

> Thirteen books of my Confessions, which praise the just and good God in all my evil and good ways, and stir up towards Him the mind and feelings of me: as far as I am concerned, they had this effect on me when I wrote them, and they still do this, when I read them. What others think is their own business: I know at least that many of the brethren have enjoyed them, and still do.
>
> (435, citing *Retractiones*, II, 32)

Montaigne

As Augustine invented the genre of confessions, so Michel de Montaigne (1533–92) established the essay genre with his massive collection of *Essays*. Unlike Augustine, he did not train for a literary career. The eldest surviving son of a Bordeaux nobleman, Montaigne received a good education in classics; his doting father, Pierre, even hired a non-French speaking Latin tutor to ensure that his son achieved an early mastery of that language. He then sent Michel to study law so that Michel could take over the father's role as magistrate, a post Montaigne assumed but that soon evolved into a local parliament position. There Montaigne met the love of his life. It was not a woman but a brilliant young intellectual and fellow parliamentarian two years older than Montaigne, Etienne La Boétie, who had already written a remarkable treatise of political theory and was enchanted with the ancient quest of the philosophical life, which he interpreted in a largely Stoic sense of virtue and courage in facing life's hardships, particularly death. Through their close friendship, he introduced Montaigne to this quest while facing an early death (at 33) with admirable bravery and generosity. Giving Montaigne his immense library and unpublished writings, La Boétie also left him horribly grief-stricken and miserably lonely. After seeking relief by plunging into carnal love affairs, Montaigne agreed to his father's wish that he marry and that he translate a fifteenth-century Latin book in natural theology by a Catalan monk, Raymond Sebond.

Montaigne inherited his father's estate in 1568 and busied himself with writing as a distraction from mourning, publishing prefaces both for the Sebond translation and for six different books of La Boétie. Three years later, after retiring from public life and sequestering himself in his study filled with the books of his dead friend and "finding [himself] entirely destitute and void of any other matter," Montaigne decided to determine and test (essay) his own beliefs by examining them against the opinions of ancient and contemporary experts (Montaigne 1965: 278). Hence, he named his project *Essays*, publishing his first two essay volumes in 1580 and a third volume in 1587, altogether totaling 107 essays. Without adding any new ones, he continued to revise and add material to his essays for the rest of his life, such additions amounting to "about one-quarter of the whole work in total length" (Frame 1965: xii).[4] The *Essays* proved immensely popular and helped Montaigne rise from a local figure to a national celebrity close to centers of cultural and political power in Paris, and someone who was apparently involved in crucial mediations between the warring Catholic and Protestant factions in a fractured France (x–xi). There was surely more to Montaigne's life than his self-study in writing, but he presents his public activities as irrelevant to his real identity, reversing the philosophical life's ancient adage of *facta non verba*. "My actions," he claims, "would tell more about fortune than about me"; they are "only details," not his lived, essential being that forms the object of his writerly project of philosophical self-knowledge. "It is not my deeds that I write down; it is myself, it is my essence" (Montaigne 1965: 274).

This was not the only reversal of philosophical doctrine that Montaigne proposed. Part of Montaigne's abiding appeal is his fresh frankness in deflating stale dogma and his colorful, concrete, wittily paradoxical, and humorous style in doing so. Though renowned as a skeptic, he remained a loyal Catholic, with more apparent faith in the goodness of divine providence than in the powers of human reason. Montaigne's early essays often involve an appreciative examination of classical philosophical themes, such as those that focus on the virtue of bravely facing death, for example, in essays entitled: "That our happiness must not be judged until after our death" and "That to philosophize is to learn to die" (a paraphrase of Socrates in *Phaedo*) (Montaigne 1965: 54, 56). Such philosophical ideals were very dear to La Boétie, and Montaigne's essays likely began as a substitute for intimate intellectual dialogue with his beloved, heroically departed friend. "I leave it to death to test [*essay*] the fruit of my studies. We shall see then whether my reasonings come from my mouth or from my heart," Montaigne writes and then continues: "The goal of our career is death. It is the necessary object of our aim … Premeditation of death is premeditation of freedom. He who has learned how to die has unlearned how to be a slave" (55, 57, 60). However, by critically examining these established philosophical ideas through the reflective and somatically engaged art of writing (rather than merely mentally reviewing them), Montaigne comes to his own very different view: "My trade and my art is living" (274). Philosophy's project of self-knowledge and self-care, he ultimately concludes, should be more concerned with learning how to live, and should affirm other ways of living besides those that focus on death and that elevate martyrs (whether stoical pagans or ascetic Christians) as their defining exemplars.

The *Essays* reveal how the art of writing figures centrally in Montaigne's evolution as a thinker. He needed writing to compensate for his avowed weakness of memory. Augustine lamented the general limitations of human memory, but Montaigne claimed his own was exceptionally feeble. "There is no man who has less business talking about memory. For I recognize almost no trace of it in me" (21). Enduring written texts enabled the examination of prior thoughts (of others and himself) that his memory could not sustain for review. Less burdened with memories, a mind had more space for invention and was less likely to dwell on past slights and disappointments.

Writing provided not only a channel to organize the stream of fleeting thoughts in Montaigne's volatile, forgetful mind but also a mirror for critically examining and reforming himself, a substitute for the dialogical regard of an intimate friend like La Boétie. Early in his project, Montaigne complains his melancholy mind "gives birth to so many chimeras and fantastic monsters, one after another, without order or purpose, that in order to contemplate their ineptitude ... I have begun to put them in writing, hoping in time to make my mind ashamed of itself" (21). Writing, moreover, is remedy of distraction from depressing thoughts. "How many times has this task [of writing] diverted me from annoying cogitations!" Montaigne exclaims, noting how it also orders the mind while entertaining it and allows him to purge anger at a safe distance from people yet in a way that can instruct them (504). Writing lets him enjoy his dreamy imagination "with some order and purpose"; "I listen to my reveries because I have to record them. How many times, irritated by some action that civility and reason kept me from reproving openly, have I disgorged it here, not without ideas of instructing the public!" (504).

Examining his thoughts in writing by testing them against the diverse opinions of famous minds provided the further advantage of self-edification because it required studying writings by the learned and wise, even though Montaigne's aim in writing was not to show off his knowledge. "I have not studied one bit to make a book; but I have studied a bit because I had made it, if it is studying a bit to skim over and pinch, by his head or his feet, now one author, now another" in examining one's own views (505). Always humble about his erudition, talent, and wisdom, Montaigne was equally modest about his book's aims: self-depiction for the sake of better self-knowledge and self-care, with the ancillary benefit of leaving friends and family an unpretentious portrait to remember him by.

> This is for a nook in a library, and to amuse a neighbour, a relative, a friend, who may take pleasure in associating and conversing with me again in this image. Others have taken courage to speak of themselves because they found the subject worthy and rich; I, on the contrary, because I have found mine so barren and so meagre that no suspicion of ostentation can fall upon my plan.
>
> (503)

Writing has the power to reshape the self who composed it, to clarify or fix contours that had previously remained vague. Moreover, once shared, writing creates pressure to conform oneself to the image one has published of oneself, to align one's actual and inner self with the outer representation, to conform one's actions to one's words. Montaigne avows:

> In modelling this figure upon myself, I have had to fashion and compose myself so often to bring myself out, that the model itself has to some

> extent grown firm and taken shape. Painting myself for others, I have painted my inward self with colours clearer than my original ones. I have no more made my book than my book has made me – a book consubstantial with its author, concerned with my own self, an integral part of my life; not concerned with some third-hand, extraneous purpose, like all other books.
>
> (504)

More than mere mental reflection and oral speech, writing has this transformative power through engaging far deeper critical self-examination. "For those who go over themselves only in their minds and occasionally in speech do not penetrate to essentials in their examination" as one who does so in writing "so continually, so carefully" (504). Writing calls for more careful thought and engages more of one's somatic self in engaging the world; from the brain to the mouth is a far shorter path than that which extends into the writing hand that inscribes one's words on solid matter. Embodied knowledge is sturdier and deeper, "we must not attach learning [merely] to the mind, we must incorporate it; we must not sprinkle, but dye" (103).

Confuting the dominant philosophical dogma that the soul is the only true self and rightful object for self-knowledge and self-care while the body is but its limiting prison or feeble, flawed instrument, Montaigne insists, "The body has a great part in our being, it holds a high rank in it" (484). The later essays therefore provide an extremely expansive account of his somatic features, capacities, habits, and tastes, even with respect to his most private parts, proclivities, and problems (such as impotence and kidney stones). If philosophy traditionally disdains the body while focusing on the soul, Montaigne counters, "On the contrary, we must couple and join them together again. We must order the soul not to draw aside and entertain itself apart, not to scorn and abandon the body ... but to rally to the body, embrace it, cherish it, control it, advise it ... so that their actions may appear not different and contrary but harmonious and uniform"; for "nothing in us ... is purely either corporeal or spiritual" (484–5, 681).

Insisting "the mind should not pursue its appetites to the disadvantage of the body," Montaigne cannot but "hate that inhuman wisdom that would make us disdainful enemies of the cultivation of the body" (681, 849). He considers it an "injustice to set our heart against natural pleasures"; we should rather enjoy them more deeply and intelligently through "greater ... attention," by being "intellectually sensual, sensually intellectual" (849, 850, 853). Rather than following the dominant philosophical line that makes reason the determining arbiter for true self-knowledge, Montaigne declares "I judge myself only by actual sensation, not by reasoning," and often "It is my body's turn to guide my mind toward reform" (638, 840).[5] In the *Essays*' final pages, he condemns the "madness" of philosophy's desire to "escape from the [bodily dimension of] man" (856). Those who seek such superhuman sanctity and bliss doom themselves to unhappy failure, if not worse; "instead of changing into angels, they change into beasts" (856).

One reason for ancient philosophy's rejection of the body was its desire to establish the unity of self, deemed central to the project of self-care and good order for a good life. Duality of soul and body meant division, disorder, and distraction; the strife Saint Paul described as "the law in [one's] members, warring against the law of [one's] mind" (Romans 7:23). Montaigne began writing his essays with the ideals of unity, stability, and heroic constancy in facing life's challenges, ideals that his friend La Boétie fervently held and bravely demonstrated. Montaigne's decision to retire from public service and family life and devote himself to writing and self-study reflects this ideal of self-unity and self-sufficiency that he dubbed "my professed principle, which is to be wholly contained and established within myself. To me it is a pleasure not to be concerned in other people's affairs and to be free of responsibility for them" (Montaigne 1965: 618). In "retreat and solitude," we "establish our real liberty" (177). Physical isolation does not suffice for focusing on self-cultivation; "we must get away from the gregarious instincts that are inside us ... [to] repossess ourselves" (176). Rather than seeking glory in the eyes of others, "we must be valiant for ourselves"; "not care ... what I am to others ... [but] care what I am to myself" (472, 474).

Initially Montaigne affirmed a different strategy for virtuous consistency: conforming thought and action to the model of ideal exemplars, heroic figures "in whose presence even fools would hide their faults." He urged us:

> make them controllers of all your intentions; if these intentions get off the track, your reverence for those men will set them right again. They will keep you in a fair way ... to arrest your mind and fix it on definite and limited thoughts in which it may take pleasure ... That is the counsel of true and natural philosophy.
>
> (183)

However, in reviewing the lives of noble heroes to determine his own path of self-care, Montaigne finds they suggest no single, unified, consistent direction. In both words and actions "they commonly contradict each other"; even the same person's thoughts and actions show inconsistency (239). He also realizes that ancient philosophy's heroic tone of strenuous ascetic transcendence through extreme "effort and tension of the will" does not really suit his own personality, which lacks such "a strong and vigorous soul" and requires "bodily comforts" (182, 770). Despite repeatedly disparaging his weaknesses, Montaigne's reflections increasingly affirm somatic pleasures and comforts as fundamental to human nature and happiness and that philosophy is intolerant and wrong in its superhuman demands. "What is the use of these lofty points of philosophy on which no human being can settle, and these rules that exceed our use and our strength?" Proposing "patterns of life which neither the proposer nor his hearers have any hope of following or ... any desire to follow" is hypocritically misleading; setting "a goal that we cannot [possibly] reach seems unjust" (756, 757).

Knowing philosophy's traditional demand for resolute consistency as crucial to virtue, that to "set [people's] lives to a certain and constant course ... is the principal goal of wisdom," Montaigne avows his own "instability" of thought and action, and condemns "irresolution [as] ... the most common and apparent defect of our [human] nature" (239–40). However, he ultimately defends and even celebrates such inconsistency as beneficial for enjoying life's diverse values and as necessary for dealing with our changing conditions, external and internal alike.

> Our principal talent is the ability to apply ourselves to various practices ... not living to keep ourselves bound and obliged by necessity to a single course. The fairest souls are those that have the most variety and adaptability ... [and] there is no way so good that I should want to be fixed in it and unable to break loose. Life is an uneven, irregular, and multiform movement.
>
> (621)

It is therefore best to cultivate flexibility in both body and soul, so that we "could both be tense and relax" (as conditions demand), to address adversity but delight in pleasure (623). The best self is "a rounded harmony, the effect of the various elements joined into a whole" (711).

How can Montaigne know himself when he "cannot keep [this] subject still" enough to hold it in focus (610)? "I do not portray being: I portray passing," he writes (611). How can he give order, stability, and unity to the self's tangled jumble "of various and changeable occurrences, and of irresolute and ... contradictory ideas" (611)? How to seize for study and improvement "a movement so wandering as that of our mind, to penetrate [its] opaque depths ... to pick out and immobilize [its] innumerable flutterings" (237)? Montaigne's solution is to capture, organize, and unify this motley, everchanging diversity by rendering it in writing, which records with the fixity of letters and the well-ordered attractions of literature. The changing diversities of life and consciousness are thus held together in the unitary wholeness of his single work of *Essays* with which that living authorial subject identifies. Exchanging psychological and behavioral constancy for literary identity, Montaigne claims his *Essays* are "a book consubstantial with its author," so if the book that constitutes him is a unified, ordered whole, then he himself is such a unity (504). "My book is always one," he affirms, a single whole to which he devoted his whole authorial life (736).

However, Montaigne knows the truth is never so simple. We could question the book's unity because its identity is repeatedly altered. First, its exact contents (namely, its words) undergo changes as Montaigne makes revisions and additions; "at each new edition" of the book he "allow[ed] [himself] to add ... some extra ornaments" for the sake of new buyers (736). Second, even when the words remain the same, there is no guarantee of stability of meaning. People can interpret the same words in different ways, and even Montaigne himself will not understand them the same way at different times because of different circumstances, both external circumstances and the internal state of the self. "Myself now and myself a while ago are indeed two; but when better, I simply cannot say" (736). Moreover, because of his feeble memory, he rarely is able to recall exactly what he meant when he wrote something down. The present self may not be smarter than the past self, but it is now alive, whereas the objectified self as written description is dead. The book can never be consubstantial with its author because the objectified self of autobiography is always different from the writing and reading subject. Montaigne admits the nonliving character of literary representation by describing his own textual portrayal, however complete, in terms of a dead body. "I expose myself entire: my portrait is a cadaver on which the veins, the muscles, and the tendons appear at a glance, each part in its place" (274).

Despite its multiplicities of words, meanings, and interpretive readings, writing manifests a model of unity that Montaigne can apply to his own volatile self and to others. It is a supple aesthetic unity of pattern rather than a narrow, rule-governed, rigid consistency. His essays are a sprawling assembly of diverse thoughts, contradictory opinions, and rambling digressions that lack the firm contours of solid, structured argument. But they nonetheless clearly hang together through an aesthetic unity of pattern, a recognizable style (personal, candid, unpretentious, and undogmatic), and a flexible form that sometimes edges towards, but should not be mistaken for, formlessness. Writing these meandering essays of self-study, Montaigne comes to realize the same sort of unity and order in himself. "There is no one who, if he listens to himself, does not discover in himself a pattern all his own, a ruling pattern, which struggles against education and against the tempest of the passions that oppose it," he affirms (615). "My actions are in order and conformity with what I am and with my condition. I can do no better" (617). The same idea of supple, unifying pattern explains how different people have very different ruling patterns without precluding a basic unity of humankind. "Each man bears the entire form of man's estate," Montaigne asserts, thus justifying the more-than-personal relevance of his extensive self-study (611). This flexible notion of a shared yet varied human *Lebensform* ultimately provides Montaigne an evaluative criterion for the art of living: "The most beautiful lives, to my mind, are those that conform to the common human pattern, with order, but without miracle and without eccentricity" that departs too monstrously from life's basic form (857).

Central to that basic form is linguistic communication and the social life that language both requires and promotes. If Montaigne originally advocated self-isolation for his project of self-study through writing, that project's essential tool of language already implied its social character. So did the project's impetus – the grief of losing the cherished company of his adored friend, intensified by the loss of his beloved father. One aspect of the "profit that I derive from writing about myself," Montaigne declares, is the "hope ... that if my humours happen to please and suit some worthy man before I die, he will try to meet me ...; for the sweetness of harmonious and agreeable company cannot be bought too dearly, in my opinion. Oh, a friend!" (749–50). "My essential pattern is suited to communication and revelation," he ultimately admits (625). "No pleasure has any savor for me without communication," which explains why he could enjoy his solitude only by writing his essays, not only for himself but also for others, avowing that "He who lives not at all unto others, hardly lives unto himself" (754, 769). The art of writing is crucial to the communicative pleasure of Montaigne's philosophical speculations, which he savors even in his solitude. Artful prose meditations can harbor the expressive pleasures of poetry. Indeed, noting Plato's use of myths and fictions, Montaigne claimed that "philosophy is but sophisticated poetry," offering "not what is ... but the most plausible and pleasant thing it forges" through speculative *poiesis* (401).

Wordsworth

In modern times the philosophy/literature divide grew deeper through the professionalization of philosophy as a university discipline devoted primarily to scientific ideals, but important thinkers continued to blur the boundaries through philosophical lives and works of genius. Prophet of Romanticism and second only to Shakespeare and Milton in the ranks of English bards, William Wordsworth (1770–1850) defined himself as a philosophical poet, devoting most of his life to composing a long philosophical poem that he never completed. Unlike Augustine and Montaigne, he was orphaned at an early age, exiled from his beloved Lake District home, and obliged to live in a series of different places before returning to settle permanently in his native rustic haven, which he preferred to any urban cultural center. Poetically proclaiming its simple virtues and domestic tranquility along with its inspirational natural beauty and sublime spirituality, Wordsworth gradually found his public identity linked to his native region as "the great captain" of "the lake poets," making him a local icon of national and international interest (Gill 1989: 301).[6]

If his multiple displacements as a youth spurred a longing for home, it also created a taste for wandering and travel. One summer during his student years at Cambridge, Wordsworth defied his family by taking an extensive walking tour through France, Switzerland, and Germany whose key focus was crossing the Alps. In 1791–2, he returned to revolutionary France, where he fell in love with a woman four years his senior, made her pregnant, and fled to England shortly after their daughter's birth but without witnessing it. He saw neither mother nor child again until 1802 as he prepared to marry Mary Hutchinson, who hailed from his home region and who, together with his sister Dorothy (a literary talent herself), provided the domestic stability and affection that nurtured Wordsworth's productivity. This included the women's exhausting labor of making fair copies of his extensive manuscripts. The dual loves of stable home and wandering travel were constants of Wordsworth's adult life that he skillfully reconciled by richly combining them (along with other contraries) through his writing, not only in poetry but in essays, letters, and travel guides. Having determined in his late twenties to make poetry his vocation, Wordsworth carefully and resolutely labored to identify work and life. He gained continued inspiration from visiting and revisiting stirring landscapes that took on added meaning through their presence in his writings. Wandering was both pleasure and research, as Wordsworth allegedly often composed while walking outdoors. A sturdy traveler and robust walker well into his later years, he made a 5-month trip through Europe at age 67 and scaled the highest mountain in his region at 70.

Like Augustine, Wordsworth had a somewhat wayward youth and fathered a child out of wedlock. He also shared with Augustine a rigorous schoolboy education in literature and precocious literary success, publishing his first poem at the age of 17 in *The European Magazine*. But Wordsworth failed to distinguish himself in studies at Cambridge, not even bothering to read for the Honours degree. We do not know the extent of his university philosophical studies, but he acquired no specialist philosophical expertise at Cambridge. In fact, he never achieved such expertise. After returning from revolutionary France, he published in 1793 two books of poetry that received little attention, although they did enchant the slightly younger Samuel T. Coleridge, an aspiring philosopher and poet, who became his close friend and collaborator.

It was Coleridge who persistently fostered (and perhaps created) Wordsworth's ambition to be a great philosophical poet through his extraordinary enthusiasm for Wordsworth's poetic gifts and his own irrepressible desire for great philosophical poetry, which he feared he lacked the poetic talent to achieve. After collaborating with Wordsworth on the revolutionary *Lyrical Ballads* (initially published anonymously in 1798 but in later editions with Wordsworth's sole name as author), Coleridge felt Wordsworth could best poetically express the philosophy he thought they shared. Affirming Wordsworth will "hereafter be admitted as the first & greatest philosophical Poet," Coleridge further explained to him and to others that Wordsworth was "a great Poet by inspirations, & in the Moments of revelation, but ... [in contrast] a thinking feeling Philosopher habitually – [whose] ... Poetry was [Wordworth's] Philosophy under the action of strong winds of Feeling—a sea rolling high" (23 July 1803) (Gill 1989: 225, 311).[7]

Wordsworth never produced any systematic writing in philosophy and his philosophical interests seem essentially confined to a few political, moral, and aesthetic issues. Some of his prose and poetry from the 1790s (that he prudently left unpublished) expressed radical Jacobin political ideas, though in later life he strongly supported conservative views and even campaigned for Tory candidates. Fundamental philosophical fields such as ontology and epistemology did not seem to interest him; Wordsworth even proudly claimed to have "never read a word of German metaphysics, thank Heaven!" (Abrams 1986: 94). Instead, the philosophical life of self-knowledge and self-cultivation seemed to be his core philosophical concern. Both poetry and lifestyle reflect his efforts to create himself as a "chosen son" destined to enlighten and heal the world through a poetic philosophical message based on the study of his own experience and imaginative consciousness, an attitude Keats dubbed the "egotistical sublime" (Gill 1989: 1, 41).

Wordsworth's projected masterpiece of philosophic poetry bore the title *The Recluse*, evoking a meditative withdrawal to pursue the classic philosophical goal of self-knowledge, and suggesting Wordsworth as its apparent hero. Repeatedly disclosed to his friends as early as 1798, his plan for the masterwork was announced to the general public in 1814, in the "Preface" to *The Excursion*, his nine-book long poem conceived as the second of *The Recluse*'s three planned parts (the others were never completed). That "Preface" described the projected masterpiece as originating with the author's having "retired to his native mountains, with the hope of being enabled to construct a literary Work that might live, ... a philosophical Poem, containing views of Man, Nature, and Society; and ... as having for its principal subject the sensations and opinions of a poet living in retirement" (Wordsworth 1814: 21–2).

The "Preface" also announced another long poem, already completed and known to his friends but still unpublished. Wordsworth described it as a "subsidiary" and "preparatory poem [that] is biographical, and conducts the history of the Author's mind to the point when he was emboldened to hope that his faculties were sufficiently matured" to write a great philosophical poem (Wordsworth 1814: 21–2). This preliminary work, Wordsworth explained, related to the planned masterwork, like an "ante-chapel ... to the body of a gothic church," while his other poems served as auxiliary "cells" or "oratories" in the building (22). The extensive preparatory poem turned out to be Wordsworth's true masterpiece, a monument of his comprehensive *poiesis* of self-creation as a Romantic icon and exemplar of the philosophical life as poet-prophet. This work, on which he continuously labored from 1798 and which exists in 4 manuscript versions, was published posthumously (in its 14-book version) in 1850 by Wordsworth's widow, as *The Prelude: Growth of a Poet's Mind*.

Always reluctant to publish it before he successfully completed the philosophical masterpiece that would justify such a long preparatory poem on the growth of his mind, Wordsworth began writing *The Prelude* as a preliminary exercise for building up his philosophical confidence through explorations in self-knowledge. But such inquiry gradually revealed that this poet's mind was not sufficiently stocked in philosophical theory to achieve the grand philosophical poem he intended on "Man, Nature, and Society." His "Preface" of 1814 already confesses "It is not the Author's intention formally to announce a system," because he did not really have one, but (vainly) hoped that by his presenting some "clear thoughts, lively images, and strong feelings, the Reader will have no difficulty in extracting the system for himself" (Wordsworth 1814: 22).

If we can speak at all of Wordsworth having a unified philosophical system, its content is rather vague, general, and largely unoriginal. Moreover, age brought changes of ideas in what he called "the river of my mind," and he was continuously busy revising earlier poems (Wordsworth 1977: 85). Yet he strove to give his corpus a sense of architectural unity or organic wholeness by incorporating the revisions into ever new editions of his *Collected Works* that were similarly structured by grouping the poems in terms of related themes rather than chronologically. Wholeness is the essential thrust of Wordsworth's entire philosophical message. There is, he claims, a common spirit and mutual fit between the works of nature and the human mind, an infinitely creative spirit that suggests a most lofty, everlasting spiritual source. Through closer communion with nature we can better appreciate this underlying unity and spiritual power in a way that elevates and edifies us toward virtue while strengthening our faith. Moreover, through this essential unity, by learning to love the beauties of nature, we can learn to love our fellow humans. Those who live closer to nature can better appreciate this common spirit and more easily find goodness and wholeness in their lives, such wholeness being a much-desired virtue and an established aim of the philosophical life. It was clearly Wordsworth's professed aim in "The Rainbow" (a short poem that also served as an epigraph to his famous "Intimations" ode):

> My heart leaps up when I behold
> A rainbow in the sky:
> So was it when my life began;
> So is it now I am a man;
> So be it when I shall grow old,
> Or let me die!
>
> The Child is father of the Man;
> And I could wish my days to be
> Bound each to each by natural piety.
> (Gill 2008: 246)

Wordsworth claims "Poetry is the most philosophic of all writing" because it has the greatest wholeness (Gill 2008: 605). Combining thought and feeling, truth and beauty, the sensory and the spiritual, knowledge and delight, poetry's teaching is "carried alive into the heart by passion" and compels by "producing immediate pleasure" while binding with "sympathy" through "the spirit of love" (605). Indeed, "the Poet binds together by passion and knowledge the vast empire of human society, as it is spread over the whole earth, and over all time" (606). Careful readers of Wordsworth, even the most sympathetic, have noted his vision of wholeness is riven with multiple conflicts and doubts that the poet's own verse betrays and that likely denied him the confidence to articulate his vision with any clarity or systematic coherence. My focus here, however, is how the practice of writing served to advance this philosophy of wholeness, apart from merely formulating it in words.

Poetic words need not be written. Some scholars see Wordsworth as essentially critical of writing, "as a poet who doesn't write poetry" (Bennet 2003: 3). Citing his practice of composing orally, frequently outdoors in the bosom of nature and in walking to and fro, they also note the implied insistence on orality in Wordsworth's praising the poet as "a man speaking to men" (Gill 2008: 603).[8] As *The Prelude* (viii, 576) describes the "written book" as "lifeless," so "The Tables Turned" urges us to shut the book's "barren leaves" to learn instead from the living leaves of nature. "One impulse from a vernal wood / May teach you more of man, / Of moral evil and of good / Than all the sages can" (Wordsworth 1977: 338; Gill 2008: 131). Writing, however, had important advantages for pursuing Wordsworth's overarching aim of wholeness by unifying diversity. In articulating these advantages below, I understand writing in its general sense of visual verbal message: not only handmade inscriptions but also printed type.

1. Writing is a material medium but also a mental or spiritual one. Sensory in visual form and conceptual in meaning, it embraces both the outer visual shapes of words and the inner realm of thoughts they represent. Writing's visual signs not only call forth meanings in the mind but also evoke the imagined sounds of the written words. Texts thus serve both as scores for oral performance and as fully fledged literary artworks that can be appreciated for their visual form and artistic uses of inscriptional or typographical design.[9] In contrast, the sound of words does not as clearly or readily evoke the letters of the utterance.

2. Written words embrace the metaphysical complexity of uniting token and type, concrete and abstract, being both a particular material inscription and an instance of the abstract type that particular inscription exemplifies; for example, the inscription "Wordsworth" has two tokens of the type letter "o" but only one token of the type letter "s." Uttered words also exhibit token/type complexity, but not as conspicuously as written or printed texts, perhaps because the uttered token word is more fleeting and is typically less abstract by being uttered with a particular intonation or expressive character. It is significant that the word "type" also designates the printed form of writing, and this ambiguity can enrich poetic meaning, as can the visuality of typography. Wordsworth repeatedly avails himself of both these aesthetically enhancing devices. He took great pains with the visual appearance of his poems on the printed page, fussing about stanza formatting and spacing, and sometimes employing special font or italics to heighten meaning.[10] He also powerfully deploys the ambiguity of the word "type" along with that

of "character" as connoting both written inscription and abstract form or meaning, doing so in key passages of his poetry. I confine myself to four examples from *The Prelude*.

In the culminating mystical experience of the moonlit night on Mount Snowdon, the elements of nature combined to create a vision where the infinite spiritual source of the universe expresses its infinite transcendent mind (a type of majestic intellect) through the language (type) of nature. "That vision, given to spirits of the night / And three chance human wanderers, in calm thought / Reflected, it appeared to me the type / Of a majestic intellect ... the emblem of a mind / That feeds upon infinity... / In soul of more than mortal privilege" (Wordsworth 1977: 513–5). The enriching ambiguity of "type" reappears in the climactic vision of wholeness in crossing the Alps, where various elements of the perceived scene together express nature's everlasting unity both in itself and with the eternal spirit that also animates humanity. Here the "rocks," "crags," "clouds," "torrents," and "woods" "Were all like workings of one mind, the features / Of the same face, blossoms upon one tree, / Characters of the great Apocalypse, / The types and symbols of Eternity, / Of first, and last and midst, and without end" (241).[11] Like "type," the word "character" refers to writing by designating written or printed letters as one of its prime meanings, along with the meanings of "characteristic nature" or "personality" or of "persona" in a work of literature, thus reinforcing the poet's unification of nature, self, and poetic creation.

Actual written inscriptions of characters figure centrally in two other key *Prelude* visions that speak more of human sorrow than nature's beautiful consolations. London's urban miseries that surround the young poet are hardly noticed till he comes across "a blind Beggar ... propped against a wall, upon his chest, / Wearing a written paper, to explain his story" (287). Reading it, the poet's "mind turned round / As with the might of waters," and felt "as if admonished from another world," taking "this label" as an "apt type" for the gloomy "utmost we can know / Both of ourselves and of the universe" (287–9). The poet's earliest visionary spot of time, recollectingly recorded late in the poem, concerned his experience as a small child who got lost from his riding companion and came across a ruined old "gibbet-mast" where "a murderer had been hung" and his name "carved" nearby "on the turf" in "monumental letters ... The characters were fresh and visible" still, and the frightened boy "fled, faltering and faint, and ignorant of the road" till he reached a height where he perceived a view of "visionary dreariness" with only a lone female figure struggling against the wind to break the desolate "moorland waste" (481). More than the gibbet, it is the writing, "the monumental letters [that] were inscribed / In times long past," the "carved" characters, that frighteningly evoke the murderer's character and the boy's fright of loss and desolation (481).

3. Writing serves wholeness by combining past and present consciousness while also implying the future. We set down in writing thoughts that

have already come to mind and that we currently assess while we write them or read what we have just written. As the written word endures, it enables and invites future reading by oneself and by others. Wordsworth, who famously described poetic composition as "emotion recollected in tranquillity," strove in both writing and life to unite past and present experience (Gill 2008: 611). So intense was the past's "self-presence in my mind … that … often do I seem / Two consciousnesses," he claims in *The Prelude* (Wordsworth 1977: 71–3). His commitment to present-writing's revisiting of the past explains his compulsion for rewriting. Addressing the changing flow of experience and the evolution of his ideas, rewriting could ensure greater unity by "bringing his past work into conformity with his present thinking … His continual rewriting stems from a determination to treat his [past] poems as living presences and to change or discard whatever no longer seems adequate" (Gill 1989: 81).

Revisions were also crucial for presenting a unified self-image and corresponding corpus that writing's permanence would project into the future. Tormented in his early career by negative reviews, Wordsworth put his hope in future readers and therefore worked tirelessly to revise repeated editions of his collected works for posterity. He explicitly maintained that "every Author, as far as he is great and … original, has had the task of creating the taste by which he is to be enjoyed; so has it been, so will it continue to be" (Gill 2008: 657–8). A text's future readers include, of course, its author. A revisited text that needs revision can also recall and inspire positive feelings that generate renewed commitment to Wordsworth's poetic philosophical life of continued creation. "So feeling comes in aid of feeling, and … as far as words can give, / Substance and life to what I feel, enshrining, / Such is my hope, the spirit of the Past / For future restoration" (Wordsworth 1977: 483). If writing *The Prelude* began as a therapeutic tool to work up his confidence because he felt "unprepared … and diffident of [his] own powers" to produce a great philosophical poem, then writing remained a continuing therapy for facing disappointments of critical reception and other challenges of life (Grosart 1876: 165).

4. Poetry enjoys an anomalous ontological status. It is a temporal art of performance when orally uttered. But the same text that functions like a musical score defining proper recitation can be appreciated silently for its meanings, without any mental mouthing of words, and with appreciation of the text's visual properties that are absent in oral performance. Literature is essentially a temporal art because it involves (whether in writing, speech, or reading) a progressive flow of words and sentences following one another. Yet in the written text this flow is fixed on the page, with all the words and sentences simultaneously present. In its forward flow, writing is like the current of life or stream of consciousness. Composing and arranging one's texts are, for serious writers, matters of organizing one's mind and ordering one's life. But because writing, unlike speech, is fixed as an inscription where successive words are simultaneously present, it enables us to read backwards

against the flow. Wordsworth could easily go back to read earlier lines of verse written at prior stages of composition, even if there were gaps of many years between readings. Moreover, with a written text, one can easily cross out or add words in revision. Wordsworth regarded memory as crucial for poetic composition, and writing can reawaken and extend memory.

5. In Wordsworth, as in Montaigne, life and writing were inextricably and symbiotically connected: his choice to live in the remote Lake District both inspired and confirmed his fame as a Lake poet. If his life served to validate the truth of his poetry, his poetry would confirm the truth and value of his life. Perhaps he never finalized and published the autobiographical *Prelude* because it was so closely identified with his living that he was unwilling to end it while still alive. His continuous revisions and rearrangements of his collected works (as well as his comparison of his oeuvre to a Gothic church) show his ambition to shape his work as a grand, enduring monument to his life as a distinctive individual with a particular personal history. In casting himself as the Recluse, Wordsworth embodied the philosophical ideal of retreating from the bustle of ordinary business to focus instead on self-knowledge and self-creation. Devoting his life's masterpiece to the growth of his mind, he notes "A Traveller I am, / Whose tale is only of himself … So be it" (Wordsworth 1977: 111–13). In *The Excursion*'s "Preface," he declares his personal focus to sing "Of the individual Mind that keeps her own / Inviolate retirement, subject there / To Conscience only, and the law supreme / Of that Intelligence which governs all" (Wordsworth 1949: 3). Writing proves most apt for such reclusive, subjective explorations because it is silent. It cannot be overheard nor can it obscure with noise of utterance the tacit, wordless language of nature's splendor whose "silent looks of happy things" express the majesty of the supreme Intelligence (Wordsworth 1949: 14). In the book of nature Wordsworth found "The written promise! Early had he learned / To reverence the volume that displays / The mystery, the life which cannot die; / But in the mountains did he *feel* his faith. / All things, responsive to the writing, there / Breathed immortality, revolving life, / And greatness still revolving: infinite" (Wordsworth 1949: 15–16).

No matter how silently and privately performed, writing has the wholeness of also being essentially public because it uses words whose meanings are widely shared and appear in abiding material form that is not limited to a single token text or object. Indeed, its allographic formulation can be infinitely reproduced and circulated in other tokens of the same type-text that properly presents the same words in the same order. Moreover, given Wordsworth's faith in the fundamental unity of things (and especially the simple, natural feelings and sympathies that we humans share), his own particular life (exemplifying growth of consciousness from love of nature toward love of humankind and faith in immortal spirit) can serve as an instructive exemplar for others. Wordsworth insisted he wanted "to be considered as a teacher, or as nothing"; "to rectify men's feelings, to give them new compositions of feeling, to render their feelings more sane, pure, and permanent, in short more consonant to Nature, that is, to eternal Nature, and the great moving Spirit of things" (Grosart 1876: 183, 211).

To teach beyond the reach of his voice, Wordsworth needed writing. He published his first poetry books during the Reign of Terror, and came to believe (like Friedrich Schiller) that aesthetics rather than activist politics could best reform the world by better educating human feelings. Nature was not enough; it required literary art to effect the needed edifying transformation, as he insisted in a late sonnet ("Illustrated Books and Papers," 1846) that praised both writing and print (though mourning print's vulgar, mass-market abuses):

> Discourse was deemed Man's noblest attribute,
> And written words the glory of his hand;
> Then followed Printing with enlarged command
> For thought-dominion vast and absolute
> For spreading truth, and making love expand.
> (Simonsen 2007: 67)

Kierkegaard

Denmark's most famous thinker, Søren Abaye Kierkegaard (1813–55) likewise turned to the art of writing in his struggle to find truth and to edify what he felt was an immoral and demoralizing society. As with Wordsworth and Montaigne, the core of Kierkegaard's writerly quest was the philosophical life of self-knowledge and meliorative self-care that could also somehow enlighten others. For him, as for Augustine, God was the necessary key and ultimate goal for this quest. The African bishop's prayer to God in *Soliloquies*, "Let me know myself, let me know You!" expresses the Dane's most pervasive and passionate desire (Augustine *Soliloquies* 2.1.1: 1888: 547). Kierkegaard was a devoutly religious Christian, but, precisely for that reason, a caustic critic of the church and Christian establishment, which he labelled "Christendom" in contrast to what he considered true Christianity. For him, the truth of Christianity, like all authentic religious faith, was a matter of personal attitude and action, not abstract doctrine or formal ritual.

Søren Kierkegaard was born into privilege, the seventh and youngest child of a wealthy Copenhagen merchant, Michael Kierkegaard, who started life as a poor shepherd boy and then made his fortune in the city, where he impressively educated himself while maintaining his humble habits of frugality and religious piety. Widowed shortly after his initial marriage, Michael impregnated his illiterate maidservant and then felt obliged to wed her. Despite the lasting success of this marriage, he continued to feel the guilt of its sinful origin in fornication and the anxiety of what punishment that sin would bring. This fearful guilt cast a gloomy pall over his household, and it increasingly intensified with the early death of all his seven children, except for Søren (the youngest) and the eldest son Peter (who became a theologian and Lutheran bishop).

Søren learned to combat and hide the gloom through mischievous wit and ironic, teasing humor, a survival strategy that created a deep split in personality. "I am a two-faced Janus, with one face I laugh with the other I cry," he confessed in his journal (Hannay 2001: 94). In public, he appeared a confidently affable extrovert and frivolous man-about-town, conversing gaily and wittily with people he met in cafes, theatres, and restaurants, where he ran up enormous bills that his indulgent father obligingly paid. Yet Søren prized his privacy as the privileged personal space where he could discover his true identity to guide him in the right path to unify his life and save his soul.

Tormented by self-division, Kierkegaard lamented the contrast between his mental powers and physical weakness, noting his "spirit ... [was] regrettably all too strong for [his] body" yet enabled him to "endure such a sickly state of health" that increased his melancholy (Hannay 2001: 373). Although delighting in literature, theatre, and philosophy, Kierkegaard felt obliged to direct his university studies towards a career in theology, studies which largely bored him and thus took him ten years to finish. Devoted to writing, he kept a journal and maintained a copious stream of publications beginning in his early twenties; yet he was painfully aware how deceptively hypocritical writing could be and how remote its abstractions were from the concrete truth of lived experience. He ardently loved his fiancée, Regina, yet immediately recognized their engagement was a mistake and brutally broke it off 13 months later despite still loving her, convinced that his "melancholy and sadness" and devotion to self-examination would make them both unhappy (Hannay 2001: 154).

Kierkegaard's overriding focus was the philosophical life, the existential pursuit of self-knowledge and edifying self-care. He sought to find himself and discover a unifying vision, a supreme center or telos to guide his life and heal his tormenting conflicts. Already in his student days, Søren sought such a unifying idea of personal truth, noting in his diary the need "to find that idea" in order properly "to find myself" and to direct concerted action to achieve a unity of "life in its organic wholeness" (Garff 2005: 58). "It is a question of understanding my destiny, of seeing what the Deity really wants me to do. It is a question of finding a truth that is truth for me, of finding the idea for which I am willing to live and die" (58). His first book, a work of literary criticism, defines such an idea as "a life-view" and argues that good literature should express such unifying visions of life. Good philosophers, moreover, should consistently live by their respective life-views, proving their particular life ideas through action rather than merely in words. Praising Socrates (the focus of his dissertation on irony) for having "only one [such view], which was absolute" and absolutely affirmed through martyrdom, Kierkegaard rebukes contemporary philosophers who "have many thoughts" but without an unwavering unified focus and proof in action (Kierkegaard 1936: 6).

Kierkegaard's posthumously published retrospective of his "Work as an Author" insisted that "the Lord Jesus Christ" was the only teacher he really believed in, but he nevertheless called Socrates his "teacher" because of Socrates' teaching method, even though the Greek was not "a Christian" (Kierkegaard 1962: 41). This is paradoxical because Socrates (and Jesus) did not teach by writing. Neither published any written texts; they lived rather than wrote their life-views. Kierkegaard (who loved paradox) was, in stark contrast, a prolific, indeed, compulsive writer. Writing formed not only his public identity, but was also how he defined himself and his life in his private journal entries. "Only when I write do I feel well"; "once I decided to stop writing," but could not, as "writing is my true life" (Kierkegaard 1993: 52, 139). Wanting his diverse writings to reflect his ideal of unity, Kierkegaard engaged in "revising some of his older journals" to ensure "that his whole authorship should demonstrate the unity whose lack he had always criticized in others and had long worried about in his own person" (Hannay 2001: 357).

Although more often studied by philosophers and theologians than by literary scholars, Kierkegaard identified himself as a literary artist, more specifically a poet. "I am essentially a poet," and "I became a poet," after "my father died," he declares, and then continues, "[Given] my decided religiousness, this *factum* [of becoming a poet] was for me at the same time a religious awakening ... in such a way that this thing of being a poet was essentially irrelevant to me" for the deepest level of identity (Kierkegaard 1962: 80, 83–4, 160). In other words, "in this thing of becoming a poet I did not recognize myself in a deeper sense, but rather [found this deeper self] in the religious awakening" (84). Moreover, "because I am nevertheless essentially a poet; but ... little more than a poet, I am essentially a penitent; but of this I cannot speak" (Kierkegaard 1962: 160). Here again, Kierkegaard's writing is wrapped in paradox. Although "writing is [his] true life" and he is "essentially a poet," he claims that nevertheless writing and poetry are not the real truth of that true life, nor its ultimate aim or calling. Instead, the truth of his message and life is something of which he cannot possibly write or speak. The crucial core of this paradox is Kierkegaard's recognition of a profound gap between existential truth and verbal discourse, coupled with the recognition that writing is his only effective method to acquire and sustain that truth. But "one should not think slightingly of the paradoxical," he claims, "for the paradox is the source of the thinker's passion, and the thinker without a paradox is like a lover without feeling: a paltry mediocrity" (Kierkegaard 1936: 29).

We can better appreciate Kierkegaard's paradoxes of writing by exploring more closely his concept of the philosophical life. Its quest for self-knowledge and a unifying life-view had the further aim of self-improvement.

Avowing "I do want very hard to perfect myself," he prayed, "God ... let me live and improve myself" (Kierkegaard 1993: 110; Hannay 2001: 92). What, then, is the self for Kierkegaard? Combining enduring identity with change, "The self is the conscious synthesis of infinitude and finitude which relates itself to itself, whose task is to become itself, a task which can be performed only by means of a relationship to God. But to become oneself is to become concrete," and the aim in its continuing "process of becoming" is to become "its own self" rather than a bland, abstract, commonality (Kierkegaard 1941: 44). Although all persons have a self, a person's self is like "life itself ... not something abstract but something extremely individual" (Hannay 2001: 15).[12]

Against the dominant Hegelianism of his time that identified truth and actual reality with the conceptual and mediating rationality of mind (expressed in the famous dictum "What is rational is actual; and what is actual is rational," Hegel 1991: 20), Kierkegaard instead located human reality in the immediacy of the individual's experience, in terms of its personal, felt existence with its inner subjectivity and wordless affect. Without denying the external world, Kierkegaard located the self's subjective inner life as the true locus of both personal reality and ethics that together form the core of the philosophical life and, more particularly, of his own philosophy, even in its deeply religious dimension. Like Augustine, Kierkegaard believed one needs divine help to know the truth of one's subjective self and to orient its will and actions to serve God. "Subjectivity is truth; subjectivity is actuality," he claims, and "only in subjectivity is there decision" that defines the ethical (Kierkegaard 2010: 171, 288). "The ethical deals with particular human beings" who have internal subjectivities, and since "the internal cannot be observed by someone outside," the ethical "can be realized only by the individual subject, who is then able to know what lives within him" by feeling it (268). This "actuality ... cannot be known just by being thought, since it is his own actuality" that the subject grasps from within, from the immediacy of felt existence, not through the abstractions of discursive thought (268). "The actual individual, after all, is indeed in immediacy" of subjective existence, not the generality and abstract ideality of language and rational thought (362).

"What actuality is cannot be put in the language of abstraction," Kierkegaard argues, because the immediacy of concrete existence has the felt, wordless passion of living, which defies reduction to language and rational thought (263). As "Existing ... is impossible without passion," so it is likewise impossible to grasp one's actual concrete existence without such affect (260). "All existence problems are passionate, for existence, when one becomes conscious of it, yields passion. To think of them without passion is not to think of them at all, to forget the point that one is oneself existing" (294). In contrast to philosophy's traditional objective, abstract thinker, Kierkegaard affirms an existential subjective thinker. "The subjective thinker's task is *to understand himself in existence*," that is, "concretely, in terms of being this particular existing human being" (294–5). "He does not abstract from existence ... In all his thinking, then, he includes the thought that he is someone existing" with passion and immediacy, with actual goals and concrete needs of action (294).

Fighting the flood of Hegelian texts touting knowledge through the mediation of rational concepts, Kierkegaard complains that "everyone writes books in which immediacy is cancelled, while no one breathes a word about how then to go about existing" (291). In contrast, he celebrates the style of concrete existential philosophy embodied in the ancient Greek ideal of the philosophical life. "To understand oneself in existence was ... to live like a Greek philosopher, i.e., expressing existentially what he would have to call his life-view, and entering existentially into it" (295). Philosophy here is an art of living, an aesthetics of existence in action. "The subjective thinker is not a scholar, he is an artist. To exist is an art" that can be ethically regulated and thoughtfully directed (294).

Philosophy, however, cannot simply be literary art. Words are inadequate to the truth of existential thinking because they partake of the abstraction and ideality of language. Rather than seeing "flesh and blood as being man's enemy," Kierkegaard claims to be "more and more inclined to look upon language ... as a still more dangerous ... enemy of man. There was, after all, something very true in that ancient view that character training begins with silence (Pythagoras)" (Bigelow 1987: 89).[13] Propositional statements cannot capture the concrete immediacy of experience; words are too general to express all the qualitative nuances of the subject's lived, felt experience. Still worse, written discourse typically pretends to have the capacity to capture and communicate this concrete existence. Readers typically mistake an author's writings for the attitudes, feelings, and beliefs the author actually has as a concrete subject. Moreover, by projecting (even unwittingly) this illusion, authors may come to believe it themselves and thus deceive themselves as well as others.

Kierkegaard inveighs against the deceptive ways that allegedly devout words depart from the true Christian piety. "Sermons as we know them today [are] ... in complete disaccord with Christianity," whose truth "can be communicated only by witnesses, i.e. by men who existentially express what they proclaim, realize it in their lives" (Kierkegaard 1993: 180). Hence, Kierkegaard frequently affirms the virtue of silence with respect to one's inner life and subjective truth. He "understood silence as [his] religious duty," because his expression of faith should be "the pious and silent accord" of appropriate action in which one demonstrates "one's thinking in his own existence ... [which] means action in life ... Only the ethical thinker, by acting, can safeguard himself against communicating illusions" (Kierkegaard 1962: 85; Kierkegaard 2010: 206; Kierkegaard 1993: 112).[14] Action, however, cannot really communicate the subject's inner truth because, for Kierkegaard, an action's meaning is defined by its intention, which remains within the inwardness of subjective consciousness. The same "external action" can be virtuous or not depending on the inner intention that motivated it, the "internality" of the person's "willing with all the passionate resolve of his subjectivity" (Kierkegaard 2010: 284, 286).

Realizing how unsuitable writing was for communicating his existential truths and religious views, Kierkegaard planned to abandon writing altogether and become "a country parson," expressing his faith in action. But this "cure" could not work because "the urge of productivity in [him] was so great that [he] could not do otherwise" than continue writing (Kierkegaard 1962: 86). The contradiction remained: how could he express through writing his personal existential truth, if writing, because of its abstract, impersonal ideality of meaning, is essentially inconsistent with that concrete, subjective, lived experience? Kierkegaard's strategy was to embrace, rather than flee, this paradox, and others.[15] The way to communicate a subjective truth incapable of being truthfully conveyed through direct statement is to convey it through falsehood and deceptive indirection. By "the use of indirect communication" and dialectical deception, one brings one's reader to grasp the ineffable subjective truth in her own existential "self-activity of appropriation," thereby incorporating that truth into her living experience of "inwardness" (Kierkegaard 1962: 58; Kierkegaard 2010: 203). Eschewing "direct attack" because "it is impossible ... to compel a person to accept an opinion," "the indirect method" works "dialectically." First, it captures the reader's interest by presenting ideas that are familiar and attractively engaging for those readers (although the author knows these ideas are "illusion") (Kierkegaard 1962: 25, 35, 40). Then it gradually leads its readers to grasp for themselves the fallacy of these initially attractive ideas and thereby evoke experientially the truth of the contrasting reality that the author seeks to convey.[16]

Kierkegaard explains his own authorial career in these deceptive, dialectical terms. Although already committed to his religious perspective, he began by writing popular and engagingly roguish aesthetic works as "only a means of communication" to gain attention (Kierkegaard 1962: 33). He also falsely presented these aesthetic texts as authored and edited by persons with strange, often amusing names or pseudonyms, even though Copenhagen cognoscenti soon realized Kierkegaard was the real author. As he avowed, "from the point of view of my whole activity as an author, integrally conceived, the aesthetic work is a deception, and herein is to be found the deeper significance of the use of pseudonyms," namely that the deception is playful and imaginatively beneficial rather than a malicious lie (39). Indeed, it is a poetic falsehood for the sake of truth.

> One can deceive a person for the truth's sake, and (to recall old Socrates) one can deceive a person into the truth. Indeed, it is only by this means,

> i.e. by deceiving him, that it is possible to bring into the truth one who is in an illusion.
>
> (39–40)

This dialectical indirect method with its use of fanciful pseudonyms is why writing, for Kierkegaard, can convey the truth better than oral discourse. Because writing enables more deception and indirection by allowing the author to hide behind multiple pseudonyms and levels of textuality (metatexts and paratexts), it can provide more (and more complex) indirect communication than an individual could ever achieve in direct oral expression where statements are directly, transparently perceived with, and attributed to, the actual person who utters them.

This distinctive method of expressing existential subjective truth through indirect, complex, writerly communication involving multiple textual layers and falsehoods has rendered Kierkegaard an admired influence on both existential and postmodern philosophy. Writing served Kierkegaard's project of philosophy as an art of living in other important ways. Having inherited enough wealth from his father, he did not need to write to earn his living, but writing was nonetheless a life necessity, a therapy with multiple functions for psychological health to "keep [himself] alive" (Kierkegaard 1993: 59). It provided an outlet for the silent, private, subjective thinker to unburden himself from his lonely, gloomy thoughts by externalizing them on the page. When Kierkegaard tried to stop writing, his "melancholy ... gained in scope" (139). Writing also provided temporary escape from that doleful self by affording distraction; he could forget himself in the imaginative fictions he invented – and particularly in the imaginary identities and discourses of his pseudonymous authors and editors. "Only when I write do I ... forget all of life's vexations, all its sufferings, then I am wrapped in thought and am happy. If I stop for a few days, right away I become ill, overwhelmed and troubled" (52). Writing, moreover, had the therapeutic, poetic power to transfigure agonies into stylish texts that provided a measure of aesthetic solace rather than mere escape.

Kierkegaard deployed multiple forms of writing in his pursuit of philosophy's core aim of knowing and improving the self. If his diary journals provided the most immediate exercises of written self-examination, then the pseudonymous aesthetic discourses enabled him to develop and express to the public a range of life-views very different from his own gravely earnest Christian outlook, while also exploring an entertaining variety of literary styles and genres. These forms include aphorisms, treatises, diaries, sermons, letters, collected papers, "a dialectical lyric" (Kierkegaard 2003), and even a book of prefaces to books that did not exist. There were also the solemn religious volumes of *Edifying Discourses* that he signed in his own name. Together these diverse forms of writing enabled Kierkegaard to find and improve himself as a deeply religious Christian with a singularly committed life-view. The wayward aesthetic writings, Kierkegaard argued, were crucial to his "upbringing" by instructing him in alternative life-views whose unavoidable problems and limitations confirmed his choice of Christianity. In exploring those views, he confessed to be "like a spy in a higher service, the service of the [Christian] idea ... I am a spy who in his spying, in learning to know all about questionable conduct and illusions and suspicious characters, all the while he is [putting] ... himself under the closest inspection" (Kierkegaard 1962: 87). All this was in "service to the cause of Christianity," Kierkegaard maintained, because one must go "out of another thing in order to become a Christian," decisively embracing the Christian view by choosing it *over* its rivals; and this meant exploring and rejecting competing aesthetic and ethical life-views, while being enriched and "educated by the process" (96).

Another way the pseudonymous aesthetic writings served his Christian life-view and philosophical art of living was by protecting his privacy and silence as an existential subject. Intensely averse to his true inner self being misunderstood by others, Kierkegaard saw the pseudonymous writings as a way he could hide his private self while still being able to share his imaginative ideas and indirect communications with the public. Kierkegaard indeed claimed:

> in the pseudonymous books there is not a single word by myself. I have no opinion about them except as third party, no knowledge of their meaning except as reader, not the remotest private relation to them, that being impossible in a doubly reflected communication.
>
> (Kierkegaard 2010: 528)

By this he meant that not only the compiled texts in these books but also the different compiling editors who prefaced those texts are not Kierkegaard himself but only "poetically actualized" personalities drawn from his imagination and whose prefaces "are their production ... as are their *names*" (527–8). Claiming "no knowledge of their meaning except as reader," Kierkegaard insists these texts have nothing at all to do with "what and how I am in my innermost being" (528). Instead, the pseudonymous writings provide a crucial camouflage of distracting noise to hide and protect his existential subjective self.

Kierkegaard highlights this use of his poetic and dialogical gift (an ability "to converse and talk with any man") as enabling him to conceal his true inner character of silent, religious devotion.

> I was granted a gift, and in such proportions that I may call it genius – this is my gift of being able to converse and talk with any man. This happy gift was granted to me to hide that I am unquestionably the most silent man in the present age. Silence concealed in silence is suspect,

> arouses suspicion ... But silence concealed in a most striking talent for conversation – that, now, is real silence.
>
> (Bigelow 1987: 89)

This strategy of deceptive concealment was not a frivolous game for aesthetically savoring the prankish pleasures of duping the public. Instead, it served his religious asceticism of purification through pain. For Kierkegaard "this unlimited freedom of being able to deceive" and hide oneself through writing "allowed [him] to be absolutely alone with [his] pain" (Kierkegaard 1962: 79). He welcomed such suffering as a route to eternal salvation in the afterlife. "I was very early initiated into the thought that to conquer means to conquer in an infinite sense, which in a finite sense means to suffer," he wrote (78). With God as his only real witness, the purifying suffering was more complete, as "there was no comfort or help to be looked for in others" (79).

Carried to its ultimate logical conclusion, Kierkegaard's view of the finite, ever-changing, existential subject would imply that even the texts he composed and signed in his own name cannot express the concrete existential truth of his actual living self. Those texts are simply the remains, traces, or past products of bygone moments in his stream of consciousness, not the expression of current, actual existential subjectivity. They are in some sense like the unfinished papers of *Nachlass* that dead authors leave behind. Any text cannot be the true expression of current existential subjectivity (which is constantly going beyond what it writes at any given moment); it is instead only a trace that remains of that subjective existence as it was actually experienced in the fleeting moment of writing. All authors have probably encountered, on some occasion, a feeling of alienation in rereading a text that they wrote but are no longer experiencing, appreciating, or understanding it as they remembered in writing it. Our memories are always limited, as is the finite perspective of one's current existential, situated state – unlike God's eternal view of things. Kierkegaard shares with Augustine and Montaigne the humble recognition of the very narrow limits of human understanding, including the meagre ability to know one's mind. He believed that one needs God's grace to know oneself and that accounts of oneself inevitably share the incompleteness of posthumous papers that were never properly finished. Kierkegaard regards this as "a feature of all authentic human production ... that it is property left behind, since it is not granted to human beings to live with an eternal view like the gods'" (Kierkegaard 1987: 153).

Nonetheless, writing is valuable for creating a form of this leftover property that, when read with critical insight, helps us appreciate our limits in revealing and communicating the truth, even the truth of one's own self. In its inability to capture concrete existential subjectivity in discursive form, writing may still somehow manage to communicate it, albeit indirectly. As Wittgenstein, who greatly admired Kierkegaard, once put it (in a letter to his friend Paul Engelmann with reference to a poem by Johann Ludwig Uhland): "if only you do not try to utter what is unutterable then *nothing* gets lost. But the unutterable will be – unutterably – *contained* in what has been uttered" (Engelmann 1967: 7).[17] Perhaps literary art's distinctive capacity for strongly evocative but indirect communication is why Wittgenstein said "philosophy ought really to be written only like *poetry* [*dichten*]" (Wittgenstein 1980: 24).[18] The next chapter explores how philosophical writers of poetry and fiction treat the enigmatic issues Kierkegaard highlighted: the impossibility of ordinary language to formulate the truth of the subject's lived existential reality, yet the power of imaginative literature to communicate indirectly a sense of that ineffable existence, albeit only through baffling logical paradox and agonizing mystery and vagueness.

Notes

1 The medical model was especially popular among the Stoics, but the Stoic Marcus Aurelius also employs aesthetic models of beauty and art for successful philosophical living in his *Meditations* (London: Penguin, 1964), 67, 165–6, 188. For an extensive, advocatory study of the medical model, see Martha Nussbaum, *The Therapy of Desire* (Princeton: Princeton University Press, 1994), which takes "as its central guiding motif the analogy between philosophy and medicine as arts of life" (Nussbaum 1994: 6).

2 With respect to some of Augustine's works cited in this chapter, besides noting my source's publication date and page number, I include original internal references of book and chapter numbers to facilitate use of other editions and translations of these works.

3 For more detailed analysis of this work, see Brian Brennan, "Augustine's *De Musica*," *Vigiliae Christianae*, 42 (1988), 267–81.

4 *Essays* is the only book Montaigne published in his lifetime; his *Travel Journal*, never intended for publication, was, however, published "almost two centuries later" (Frame 1965: x).

5 Montaigne goes so far as to challenge philosophy's conventional ideal of rational tranquility: "the tranquil state of the soul, the sedate state, the healthiest state that philosophy can acquire for her, is not her best state." The soul reaches highest in its inspired, impassioned transports, where "we improve by the privation and deadening of our reason" (Montaigne 1965: 427).

6 These quotes (from one of Wordsworth's most severe critics) are cited from the excellent biography by Stephen Gill, *Wordsworth: A Life* (Oxford: Oxford University Press, 1989), 301.

7 The first quotation is in a letter to a friend in 1804; the second from a letter to Wordsworth, 28.7.1803; S.T. Coleridge, *Collected Letters*, ed. E.L. Griggs (Oxford: Oxford, University Press, 1956), vol.2, 957 and 1034. Cited in Gill, 225, 311.

8 See, for example, Andrew Bennet, "Wordsworth Writing," *The Wordsworth Circle* 34:1 (2003), 3–6.

9 I treat this in detail in Richard Shusterman, "Aesthetic Blindness to Textual Visuality," *Journal of Aesthetics and Art Criticism*, 41:1 (1982), 87–96, expanded in *Surface and Depth* (Ithaca: Cornell University Press, 2002), ch. 9.

10 On the importance of typography, see Peter Simonsen, *Wordsworth and Word-Preserving Arts: Typographic Inscription, Ekphrasis and Posterity in the Later Work* (London: Palgrave Macmillan, 2007).

11 In being silent, *inscriptions* (unlike speech) share with natural objects the quality of "an inarticulate language" that is not pronounced but still communicates. Nature's silent but loving communication, Wordsworth insists, can teach us to love our fellow humans. "Not useless do I deem / These quiet sympathies with things that hold / An inarticulate language; for the man / Once taught to love such objects ... must feel / The joy of that pure principle of love / So deeply that ... he cannot choose / But seek for objects of a kindred love / In fellow-natures, and a kindred joy." Appendix (b) (Excerpt from manuscript of "The Ruined Cottage") (Gill 2008: 678, lines 3, 1–11).

12 This citation is from Kierkegaard's posthumous papers as translated and cited by Hannay, p. 15 (the source is Søren Kierkegaard*'s* (1909–20) *Papirer* edited by P.A. Heiberg and V. Kuhr, Copenhagen: Gyldendalske, I B2, 172).

13 From an entry of 1854 in *Papirer*, XI A 128, as cited in translation in Patrick Bigelow, *Kierkegaard and the Problem of Writing* (Tallahassee: University of Florida Press, 1987), 89.

14 It is noteworthy that some of the pseudonyms Kierkegaard deploys suggest the idea of silent withdrawal into the inward: Johannes de Silentio, Father Taciturnus, and Victor Eremita ("victorious hermit").

15 Other paradoxes include the felt "unity of the metaphysical and the contingent ... in self-consciousness," in which "I become at the same time conscious in my eternal validity, in my divine necessity, so to speak, and in my contingent finitude ... as this particular being, born in this country, at this time" and shaped by changing conditions (cited in Hannay 2001: 135). Similarly paradoxical is the existential faith in Christ's incarnation (the presence of the supernatural and eternal God being born into history as a contingent, changing person), which Kierkegaard's faith embraced as logically absurd with no attempt at rational justification.

16 Kierkegaard likens this indirect method to the famous Socratic style of dialectic midwifery. Rather than beginning by arguing for the truth he hopes to convey to his interlocutor, Socrates instead starts somewhere else where he and the interlocutor agree, and then dialectically brings the interlocutor to achieve the desired conclusion herself, just as a midwife brings the pregnant woman to issue her child.

17 Ludwig Wittgenstein, "Letter to Paul Engelmann" (April 9, 1917) quoted in *Letters from Ludwig Wittgenstein, with a Memoir by Paul Engelmann*, ed. B.F. McGuinness (Oxford: Blackwell, 1967), 7.

18 I cite here, again, from the bilingual edition of Ludwig Wittgenstein, *Vermischte Bemerkungen/Culture and Value*, ed. G.H. Von Wright (Oxford: Blackwell, 1980) but give my own translation for "*dichten*" rather than the more cumbersome, "*a poetic composition*" that appears in the published English translation. Wittgenstein's German sentence is "Philosophie dürfte man eigentlich nur *dichten*."

3 Expressing the Ineffable

Four Exemplary Philosophical Writers

This chapter explores literature's alleged power to reveal and communicate otherwise ineffable truth by considering four twentieth-century authors whose work defies the presumption of a dichotomous divide between philosophical and literary writing. We begin with a pair of influential French thinkers, Georges Bataille (1897–1962) and Maurice Blanchot (1907–2003), who wrote both narrative fiction and critical theory. They were close friends and collaborated in some publishing projects, Blanchot writing many of his most important essays in the journal *Critique* that Bataille founded and edited and that still exists today. Neither Blanchot nor Bataille held a doctorate or university position. Though largely inspired by German philosophy (especially Hegel and Nietzsche), their theorizing also shows a deep appreciation of Kierkegaard's existential thought. They affirmed the Dane's insistence on the need for paradoxical and indirect communication of deeply hidden truth, but their style of philosophical writing is, on the surface, far more challengingly opaque than Kierkegaard's invitingly flowing prose.

The other pair of authors, Bertrand Russell (1872–1970) and T.S. Eliot (1888–1965), were closely acquainted, and both are renowned for the clarity of their theoretical prose. As a visiting professor at Harvard in 1914, Russell taught Eliot (then a doctoral student in philosophy). A year later, after a hasty marriage in England and consequent break with his American family, the penurious Eliot and his unstable bride Vivienne took refuge in Russell's London flat, where the philosopher continued to play a significant but equivocal role in the couple's unhappy marriage. In different ways, Russell and Vivienne influenced Eliot's decision to give up an academic career in philosophy and become a poet, but he did complete an excellent doctoral dissertation (on the neo-Hegelian F.H. Bradley) in 1916 and continued for a time to publish articles in professional philosophy journals.[1] As Eliot's theorizing on literature, criticism, culture, politics, and religion exhibited philosophical expertise, so Russell's literary status commanded recognition. Two years after Eliot won the Nobel Prize in Literature "for

DOI: 10.4324/9780429331770-3

his outstanding, pioneer contribution to present-day poetry," Russell won the same prize for his popular essays on "varied [topics] ... in which he champions humanitarian ideals and freedom of thought" (NobelPrize.org).[2] Encouraged by the prize, Russell published his first book of fiction, a collection of short stories entitled *Satan in the Suburbs*, and he went on to publish another story collection in 1954, *Nightmares of Eminent Persons*, and then in 1961 a miscellany of essays and tales, appropriately titled *Fact and Fiction*.[3]

Although Russell and Eliot contrast sharply with Bataille and Blanchot in terms of literary style, all four authors made writing the essential tool for their philosophical lives of sustained critical inquiry into self and world. Suggesting, in different ways, how literature can communicate a deeper level of reality that defies formulation in ordinary language, they shared the view that such reality was horrifically dark, cruel, and unfathomably senseless. We consider these writers in turn.

Bataille: The Ineffable Truth of Inner Experience

Georges Bataille was among the first to introduce Kierkegaard's philosophy into French thought, and, like Kierkegaard, created amusing pseudonyms that he employed for his early erotic fictions, which the high-strung Dane would surely have described as sacrilegiously pornographic rather than aesthetic.[4] Bataille shared Kierkegaard's commitment to subjective, existential truth residing solely within the individual's immediate, affective experience. Although every human subject may have an inner life of personally felt reality, these particular, concretely felt inner states of existential experience are directly accessible only to the subject who has them and cannot be captured by ordinary discourse, which necessarily involves the abstraction and generality of conceptual language. Such inner states are extremely elusive even to the subject herself, because they only briefly appear in the fleeting lived moments of passing time. Moreover, awareness of them is usually repressed by ordinary practical thinking, which focuses our attention on enduring objects of the external world and the shared concepts of language we employ to survive and flourish in our practical pursuits.

Bataille distinguishes one such subjective state as "*inner experience*" and celebrates it as special not only in its intensity but also in providing the deepest sense of reality and experience's "extreme limit" (Bataille 1954: xxxii, 3). Because this mental state of extreme limit reaches the very depths of consciousness and is foreign to rational thought and language, it needs the pressure of extremely intense (typically violent) forms of experience to reveal its hidden truth, while likewise requiring indirect communication through special language to express it and the reality it unveils. Such ultimate, existential, experiential truth defies our ordinary notion of knowledge because it flouts the normal logic and language of discursive reason that defines both practical and scientific knowledge. It is closer to mystical vision that takes "non-knowledge to be its principle" of insight (3). Bataille explains, "By *inner experience* I understand that which one usually calls *mystical experience*: the states of ecstasy, of rapture, at least of meditated emotion" but that are "free of ties" to any religious faith – states "where anguish and ecstasy coexist" (xxxii, 3).

Instead of religion, Bataille (who abandoned his Catholic faith after training for the priesthood) substitutes literature as the purveyor of mystical experience and truth. As editor of *Critique*, he wrote (in 1947), "Today, the literary game is the quest of ultimate realities, of sacred truth, which ... ordinary (discursive) language cannot express"; although some may "want to see none of this, ... from the moment literature stopped being for religion what the servant or poor relation was to the master, it inherited religion's power and role" (Bataille 1947: 463).[5] Ten years later, he confirmed that literature absorbed "the heritage of religion" to provide "'mystical experience'" in whose "states we can see a different truth to that which is concerned with the perception of objects, or indeed of the subject, connected, as it is with the intellectual consequences of perception." However, Bataille continues, "this is not a formal truth" expressible in ordinary "coherent" discourse [*discours*] and "would be incommunicable if we could not approach it in two ways: through poetry and through the description of those conditions by which one arrives at these states. These conditions correspond decisively" with literature's central themes of love and death (Bataille 1985: 25–6).

Why are these inner states of concrete, existential lived experience so difficult to observe and impossible to express in ordinary language? What is the special character of that extreme interior state Bataille designates as inner experience; and why is literature best able to communicate it? Various obstacles thwart the observation and communication of one's inner life. For practical reasons of survival (like acquiring food and escaping predators), consciousness evolved to direct explicit attention principally to our external environment rather than the flow of our inner states and feelings, unless those feelings become especially intense or painful. Our inner feelings, moreover, are mostly too fleeting and vague for careful observation; consciousness is a continuous flow rather than a series of discrete, clearly individuated feelings or objects. That is why William James described consciousness as a *stream* rather than a *chain* composed of distinct links. Although we can identify and name some particular thoughts or feelings in that stream, these particulars are always surrounded, connected, and carried forward with a host of nameless feelings of transition in that flowing stream. Moreover, if we try to fix our attention on a particular experiential state to examine it, we find it immediately changes into something else by the very act of attending to it, just as grasping a snowflake inevitably fails by turning it into a drop of water. Attentive consciousness cannot capture immediate feelings because it transforms them.

In particular, Bataille emphasizes that the very effort to examine inner states of intensely close communion or deep communication with the world paradoxically alienates us from those experiences. Hence, such

> moments of intense communication which we experience with that which surrounds us – whether it is a matter of a row of trees, of a sunlit room – are in themselves ungraspable. We only take pleasure in them to the extent that we *communicate* [unthinkingly with them], that we are lost, inattentive. If we cease to be lost, if our attention is intensified, we cease for all that to *communicate*. We seek to understand, to capture the pleasure: it escapes from us.
>
> (Bataille 1954: 140)

The will to knowledge focuses on clear, knowable objects of thought, but this excludes our experienced but indefinable feelings related to that object, which are essential to the fullness of our communication with the object though neglected by practical and intellectual cognition. Thus, "in wanting to grasp, nothing remains in our hands but the bare object, without the impression which accompanied it. The intense release of life which had occurred, as in love, moving towards the object, losing itself in it, escapes from us, because in order to apprehend it, our attention is turned naturally towards the object, not towards ourselves" (140).

Our explicit knowledge is discursive, relying on language to individuate things and to distinguish their properties and relations. Having developed predominantly to serve practical aims requiring clarity of meaning, language relies on syntax and semantics involving discrete words with shared, general, identifiable meanings that combine into discrete sentences. In contrast, one's inner states belong to a streaming continuum and have a particular, personal feel defined by the particular conditions of the particular person at a particular time. The general word "desire" cannot do full justice to the countless, differently nuanced forms, degrees, stages, and feelings of desire that a particular person experiences subjectively. Discursive language will

> permit us to reach objects with ease, [but] attain poorly the inner states, which remain strangely unknowable to us. We have consciousness of these states, but in a fleeting fashion, and to want to stop there, to have them enter our field of attention, is, in the first instance, to want to know them, and we only become aware of them to the extent that we let go of our discursive mania to know!
>
> (Bataille 1954: 140)

Even if "we want to give our attention to what is inner, this attention slips nevertheless to the object" (140). Bataille argues that one way to dwell appreciatively in such inner states of communion is to avoid language by instead focusing on meditative "states proceeding from objects which are in themselves barely graspable (silence, breath)," but literature, despite being language, can provide another way (140). "Literature is *communication*," Bataille insists; indeed it involves communication's deeper sense of bringing us toward an underlying, almost mystical communion with one's own inner states and the world beyond the self because it breaks with the ordinary practical aims of language and knowledge (Bataille 1985: ix).

Ordinary language and the knowledge it communicates rest on the logical principle of difference. Language distinguishes subject from object; and its words and concepts derive their meaning from their differences or contrasts with each other (night and day, fast and slow, stop and go). The meaning of Tuesday is that it is not Monday, Wednesday, Thursday, Friday, Saturday, or Sunday. Constituted by differences, language projects those differences onto the world of experience – establishing a world of discrete objects that present themselves to human subjects (likewise individuated by names and linguistic descriptions) who perceive, manipulate, and communicatively address those objects and fellow humans in order to advance their particular practical projects as living, striving subjects. Language individuates objects so that we can re-identify, observe, and study them to increase our knowledge and utilize it for practical benefit. Discursive knowledge, as essentially structured by divisive difference, cannot capture the felt unity of the continuous stream of inner states of experience that the subject identifies as her living self "the existence which I am" (Bataille 1954: 110).

Such knowledge, moreover, can never achieve the deeper communication of underlying communion with the world that Bataille describes as the mystical, ecstatic truth of "non-knowledge" (Bataille 1954: 52). This "non-knowledge communicates ecstasy" because it breaks with the unhappy division of discourse and its individuated, separated knowing subject (52). "There is no longer subject-object … there is passage, communication" in which the subject-object division is "dissolved" (59). With the collapse of the subject-object contrast and the differential logic of ordinary discourse comes the dissolution of ordinary, practical sense and the divisive distinctions of discursive knowledge. In the intensity of Bataille's "inner experience," discursive difference disintegrates into ecstatic unity. The individual subject is *ec*-static by being in an intensely felt experiential state *outside* her individual, separate self-consciousness. But such ecstasy, devoid of one's normal sense of self and the world of known objects, is also a fearful distress. "Non-knowledge is anguish before all else" (52).

Literature, especially poetry, is distinctive in flouting the ordinary differential rules of language to create experiences that defy practical logic and the limits of rational meaning in order to create special, intense aesthetic experiences that highlight unity, fusion, and immediacy. These experiences transform language into something that, in practical terms, is non-knowledge or even non-sense, but that nonetheless powerfully communicates between two subjective solitudes (the composing author and the reader) to create an experiential bond that "communicates ecstasy" and suggests a deeper reality of underlying unity (Bataille 1954: 52). For Bataille, such peak aesthetic experience, like mystical experience, evokes a "divine intoxication which the rational world of calculation cannot bear"; "the intoxication of existence" in which "the isolated being *loses himself* in something other than himself," and thus momentarily escapes the world of utilitarian reason where everything is a means to some further end of life (Bataille 1985: 22, 26). From that practical perspective literature appears a childish, trivial, if not also an irresponsible or evil pursuit.

In "the prosaic world of activity," language serves the ends of action; words are signposts directing us to their real referents in order to manipulate them for our projects and future use (Bataille 1985: 43). Literature instead enables us to appreciate the words in themselves through the communicative experience they provide in the fleeting "present moment" of experiential immediacy, without regard to utility and the future (43). Literature, Bataille claims, offers "the value of 'mystical participation,'" of losing oneself in the experience of the work, where we find "the fusion of subject and object, of man and the world" (e.g. the reader or writer and the text) or, in another formulation, "the identity of reflected things and the consciousness which reflects them" (42, 44, 45). In cancelling the real existence of the objects it seizes to render them as imaginative literature, poetry "returns them to the elusive fluidity of the poet's existence" (45). It thus suggests "the identity of the world and man" (45), while affording the pleasure of release from the ordinary framework of serious, practical activity that defines human life in terms of separate individuals struggling to deal with a world of objects and particular human subjects that are experienced as separated, alienated realities.

What, then, is the informulable truth that the mystical inner experience of union reveals and that the art of literature can never fully capture but can communicate indirectly through its own forms of immediacy and fusion? By definition we cannot formulate it, but Bataille claims it reveals that the world of reason, language, and practical activity that we commonly take for our basic foundational reality is only a convenient construction, a cogent pragmatic fiction. Its function is to help us survive and to keep us busily distracted as individuals focused on practical self-interest, thus concealing from us a deeper, true reality that is discomforting, even if secretly desired. That underlying reality is the continuous, unceasing, unstructured stream of existence that is constantly changing and reshaping itself in fleeting constellations that language and practical reason organizationally differentiate as the world of things and wrongly identify with the ultimately real. True reality, Bataille claims, does not respect the basic principle of individuation that defines our world of separate objects and subjects, of distinct entities; instead, reality is a crazy streaming continuum of chaotic, changing existence, a continuity that contains and dissolves everything in its undifferentiating, flowing fusion.

> From one single particle to another, there is no difference in nature, neither is there any difference between this one and that one. There is *some of* this which is produced here or there, each time in the form of unity [that suggests a distinct enduring object], but this unity does not

> persevere in itself. Waves, undulations, single particles are perhaps only the multiple movements of a homogeneous element; they only possess fleeting unity and do not break the homogeneity of the whole.
>
> (Bataille 1954: 93)

The world of separated beings, both objects and subjects, is ultimately merely a practical fiction created by rationality's *principium individuationis* that Nietzsche earlier identified with the Apollonian aesthetic principle that seeks the clarity, order, and harmony of distinct and well-defined objects in order to overcome and conceal the frightening perception of a deeper, underlying reality devoid of such individuation. At that deeper level, the so-called world of individual things dissolves into a tissue of illusory "incessantly changing appearances" like "the veil of maya"; its presumably real objects are merely transient constellations or constructed unities momentarily separated out of the more fundamental, all-encompassing, ever-driving stream of existence, "the mysterious primordial unity (*das Ur-Eine*)" (Nietzsche 1999b: 18, 80).

A person's individual self is one such fragile, fleeting, and ultimately illusory unity. "It is true that this isolated 'being' … is the form in which existence and truth at first appeared to you. It is to this irreducible difference – which you are – that you must relate the sense of each object. Yet the unity which you are flees from you and escapes," because it is merely a series of incessantly changing appearances constructed by the flux of life through different constellations of elements that will soon dissolve in your death and be taken up into other constellations that are not you (Bataille 1954: 94). "What you are," continues Bataille, "stems from the activity which links the innumerable elements which constitute you to the intense communication of these elements among themselves. These are contagions of energy, of movement, of warmth, or transfers of elements, which constitute inevitably the life of your organized being" (94). That constellation is but a fleeting ripple in the broader continuum of life that changes rapidly "like a current or like a sort of streaming of electricity. Thus, there where you would like to grasp your timeless substance, you encounter only a slipping, only the poorly coordinated play of your perishable elements" (94). Our fear of death, the dissolution of our individual being in the primal unity, makes the revelation of that unity a frightening vision, but it is also an ecstatic one of full union and communion, *ec-stasis* in the literal sense of taking us out of ourselves.

We may sometimes get a sense of this encompassing streaming unity, because the changing constellations of elements that constitute the self are in communication not only with each other but also with the constellating elements of other temporary things in the flux. The self is a transactional entity; even the body's separating skin is a semipermeable membrane that communicates with its environment. Hence, "your life is not limited to that ungraspable inner streaming; it streams to the outside as well and opens itself incessantly to what flows out or surges forth towards it," reflecting the underlying reality of streaming continuity, and yearning to express it (94). For Bataille, the two key biological expressions of that drive toward unity are the phenomena of sexual desire and death. In erotic desire, the individual yearns to fuse one's body with another's and escape one's sense of isolated consciousness in the intoxication of frenzied, orgasmic passion (whose ecstatic combinations of self-fulfillment and self-abandonment, love and violence, pleasure and pain are emblems of an all-embracing unity that dissolves oppositions). Because death ends the separation of our particular current of life from the broad sea of existence, Bataille sees the death wish as similarly expressing a desire for the ecstasy of self-abandoning union in a larger whole. Although sexual union seems to be seeking death's nullification through the procreation of offspring (additional isolated beings), Bataille argues that even here sex is a form of death for the individual because it kills her individuality by killing its autonomous freedom with burdens of parenthood. He thus defines eroticism as "assenting to life up to the point of death," claiming that both sex and death involve the "effort to reach continuity by breaking with individual discontinuity" (Bataille 2012: 11, 144).

How does literature join sex and death as capable of communicating this vision of continuity? How can it destroy the familiar discontinuities of our rational, practical world of individual things and thus evoke experiences of both ecstatic and horrific unity? First, literature makes the horrible and rapturous experiences of erotic love and death central topics in its stories, drama, and poetry. Moreover, through its fictional character, literature annuls the reality of the world of things by using the language that designates those things to create an imaginary world that, in a sense, transforms them into unreal entities. By disengaging us from the practical world, literature allows us to savor the compelling immediacy of its own aesthetic experience whose intensity reminds us of the compelling though often hidden reality of inner feelings. Yet that aesthetic experience of the literary work can be so powerful as to challenge one's separate identity as an individual subject by fusing one's subjective consciousness with the objectivity of the work. Subject and object are fused as the reader is absorbed or lost in the work. Poetry especially suggests unity through its metaphorical fusions of sense, its unification of contrasts, its mysterious ambiguities that suggest an endless stream of possible meanings and can embrace the vast, endless expanse of the universe in a short burst of verse. Bataille explains this with four lines by Rimbaud:

> Elle est retrouvée.
> Quoi? L'éternité.
> C'est la mer allée
> Avec le soleil.
> (Bataille 2012: 25)[6]

"Poetry," Bataille continues, "leads to the same place as all forms of eroticism – to the blending and fusion of separate objects. It leads us to eternity, it leads us to death, and through death to continuity. Poetry is eternity; the sun matched with the sea" (25).[7]

Rather than poetry, Bataille wrote erotic narratives whose highly transgressive and violent content linked the ecstatic convulsions of sexual fusion with the seizures of death. In these extreme somatic experiences, as in mystical experience, individual consciousness is overwhelmed in a bursting flood of union where conventional oppositions dissolve and merge together. In the *Story of the Eye*, Bataille describes this experiential goal of "sexual licentiousness: [as] a geometric incandescence (among other things, the coinciding point of life and death, being and nothingness), perfectly fulgurating" (Bataille 1987: 33). The story's two teenage protagonists, despite many preliminary lewd acts, do not copulate until they become overwhelmingly excited over the dead body of the friend they corrupted and led to suicide. Death brings fuller union not only to them but also with that dead friend who "was closer to [them] dead than in her lifetime" (51). The narrative's climax is the simultaneous rape and murder of a young priest in which the paroxysms of orgasm and death are concurrent and indistinguishable, at least for the narrator-accomplice who helps pin the priest down.

In the short story "Madame Edwarda," Bataille's evocation of inner experience through sex and violence likewise affirms the primordial unity of opposites. He speaks of "the identity that exists between the utmost in pleasure and the utmost in pain: the identity between being and non-being, between the living and the death-stricken being, between the knowledge which brings one before this dazzling realization and definitive, concluding darkness," which ultimately suggests even the blending of meaning and nonsense (Bataille 1995: 140).

> A hidden meaning? Hidden, yes, "obviously"! ... No, I can't conceive of any "meaning" other than "my" anguish, and as for that, I know all about it. And for the time being: nonsense. Monsieur Nonsense is writing and understands that he is mad. It's atrocious. But his madness, this meaninglessness – how "serious" it has become all of a sudden! – might that indeed be "meaningful"?
>
> (159)

Bataille highlights the linking of sexual passion with death in his short novel *My Mother*. Both experiences involve intense fusion and loss of self, dissolving conventional contrasts and individuating limits into the wild, raging continuum of existence that inevitably includes the individual's death. The novel depicts how a beautiful, lasciviously transgressive young mother (of lesbian taste) genuinely loves but foully corrupts her beloved teenage son Pierre. She does so by employing the sexual seductions of two of her young female lovers, who introduce the beloved son to licentious excess that finally leads to his committing the ultimate transgressive act of maternal incest, which prompts the scheming mother to commit suicide. The earlier seductions of Pierre are the mother's indirect sexual communication to prepare him for his ultimate experience of transgressive, death-related sex. This erotic education trains him to appreciate the contraries contained in the experience of extreme passion that connects sex to death (pleasure and suffering, beauty and hideousness, tenderness and violence, joy and terror, good and evil, the personal and the impersonal). "It's too wonderful, it's too awful," Pierre exclaims in tears, as the mother instructs him that "to become delightful happiness must be tainted with poison," explaining to him that "terror was my joy ... I believe that all I love is love, and in love itself only the torment of loving" (Bataille 1995: 64–5, 73).

The violent oblivion of sexual passion, through its overwhelming of self-conscious restraint and "abolishing of limits" in the ecstasy of union, suggests the individual's final oblivion in death and thereby indirectly communicates the deeper reality of unity and flux that dissolves all individuals along with all distinctions and contrasts (116). We learn that "sensual pleasure and death have the same dignity – and the same indignity – the same violence and nevertheless the same sweetness" (86). Love's "'suffering is a delight. But it's suffering nevertheless' ... Nausea, happiness ... blending indistinguishably" (115). In sexual ecstasy we "'die' ... [because its] intensity and intimacy of a sensation open up an abyss in which everything is lost, like the deep wound which opens up at death" (104). Although writing cannot match sex and dying in communicating the existential feel of an extreme limit experience of self-abandonment, it can, on occasion, somehow succeed in suggesting or pointing toward it. As the mother explains, "Writing to you, I am made to realize how impotent words are, but I know that in the long run, despite their impotence, they will get through to you" (91).

Blanchot: An Inexpressible Reality beneath the Space of Literature and Language

Maurice Blanchot avows this impotence of words to capture the depths of experience and existence, while nonetheless affirming literature's particular power to communicate them indirectly. Because he led a reclusive writer's life for most of his adult years, our knowledge of Blanchot comes largely through his literary work – the essays, book reviews, and works of fiction, which mainly focus on the nature and function of literature and language.[8] After studying philosophy in Strasbourg (together with Emmanuel Levinas), he essentially made writing his philosophical life. In his study of Kierkegaard, Blanchot affirms the Dane's view that conceptual language cannot express the singularity of the subject's concrete individual existence for which "there is no direct communication possible," but which can be evoked by literary means, through a "method of indirect expression" in which what is said "appears like the sign of that which must be hidden" (Blanchot 2001: 19–20).

The individual's barren solitude is a key theme for Blanchot, an expression of the essential human condition of isolating subjectivity that nonetheless seeks to communicate, even when communicating nothing more than this solitude and emptiness. This isolation is epitomized by "the act of writing" that the author does alone. Even if longing for potential readers, "he aligns himself with the solitude that it is his destiny to apprehend in the very act of writing" (Blanchot 2001: 2, 10). "The writer is not free to be alone without expressing that he is ...; and it is even in the manner of his expression that he coincides best with the inexpressible nothingness that he has become" (2). One way that literature can indirectly signify the singularity of personal existence is through its own uniqueness. Unlike ordinary language, which is essentially general and instrumental for signifying and handling things that could be designated with other word formulations, literary meaning is unique and cannot be paraphrased.

> Poetic meaning is not a matter of some generalization for which many means of expression are possible and that can be applied to any number of cases. It works only once, and it makes the system of images, symbols, and consonances that is inextricably associated with it untransferable. It belongs to the category of the Unique.
>
> (109)

If we respect the human individual as an end in itself rather than as a mere instrument or tool to use for other things, then a literary work is similarly appreciated for its own sake, differing from the "everyday use [of] language [as] an instrument" (109). The literary work "demands a total acquiescence to the unique form that it proposes. The sense of the poem is inseparable from all the words, from all the movements, from all the accents of the poem. It exists only in this ensemble" (108). Moreover, the experience the work delivers is unique; indeed, unique every time it is read; its meaning is not the property or the tool of its creator. "He does not hold its meaning, its privileged secret ... Author and reader are equals with respect to the work and in it. Both are unique" (Blanchot 1989: 227). As concrete individual human existence has an inextricable, unique materiality that we care for and cherish, so we appreciate how the words of literary works (unlike ordinary language) insist on their sensuous properties or "material value, and ... the force they possess to attain the depths of reality" (Blanchot 2001: 110).

For Blanchot those depths lie deeper than what ordinary language can express or what even literary language can directly formulate. Yet literature can communicate this elemental reality indirectly, by its "power to evoke, to call forth mysteries that it cannot express, to do what it cannot say, to create emotions or states that cannot be represented" that connect "to profound existence" and "the understanding of the situation of man" (Blanchot 2001: 110). Literature conveys this deep, enigmatic reality partly through its own obscure, inscrutable nature. Like human individuals, literary works have their "opaque profundity," unfathomable mysteries and complexities that defy clear formulation; even when we think we understand them, there is always something "which escapes comprehension, which is unascertainable" (Blanchot 1989: 223, 228). A powerful literary work can evoke a state in us "that we identify ... with the original feeling [of pure existence itself], the one that we experience when we touch the deepest part of ourselves" (Blanchot 2001: 135).

Crucial for literature's power to communicate the depths of reality is its highlighting the expressive essence and meaning of language itself. Literature is unlike ordinary practical discourse where language is an instrument to deal with other things, where it functions as a transparent sign to indicate those other things, where it renders itself invisible so as not to distract us from those things and thus enables us to deal with them more efficiently by not calling attention to itself as language. Instead, Blanchot insists, literature self-consciously demands attention to itself as language, to the particular words of the work, to their sensuous, aesthetic qualities and their forms and styles of meaning, appreciating them for their own sake rather than for the things they refer to (which anyway are typically nonexistent fictions). Thus, "in the poetic act language stops being an instrument and reveals itself in its essence, which is to found a world, to make possible the authentic dialogue that we ourselves are, and, as Holderlin says, to name the gods" (Blanchot 2001: 109). By highlighting its creative power to produce a literary work that "exists in itself as ensemble of sounds, cadences, metrics" through "the linking of forces that it symbolizes, [language] reveals itself as the foundation both of things and of human reality" (109). Through its formative essence, its powers of individuating and naming objects, actions, and qualities and of relating them to each other, "Language is what founds human reality and the universe," effectively creating the world of things and people (and even gods) who are present and known only through language's constitutive designations and descriptions (167).

Blanchot, like Bataille, follows Nietzsche, however, in affirming a reality deeper than the universe of individual things and truths that language founds and defines, a reality far more unfathomable and obscure, even deeper than language itself. Although this reality defies linguistic formulation, literature can evoke it paradoxically because it negates, through a double movement of negation, what we typically take for reality. Language first negates the ordinary reality of things, their existential quiddity or substantial "whatness," by turning them into linguistic expressions – names or designating descriptions that are symbols detached from the things they symbolize. Blanchot explains, "when I say, 'This woman' ... my language means that this person, who is here right now, can be detached from herself, removed from her existence and her presence" and converted into an abstract linguistic sign that can refer generally to any woman in the appropriate circumstances (Blanchot 1995: 323). In ordinary language this negation of the material thing preserves the reality of a clearly signified concept – the idea of a real woman who is indicated as really and truly present by the demonstrative adjective "this." However, literature's language of fiction performs the further negation by which the linguistic sign does not even symbolize the idea of a really existent person but simply functions in the weaving of an alternative, fictitious world in contrast to the real world of individual things, persons, and events. Here language creates a separate realm beyond the ordinary world of particulars and practical life, a realm Blanchot identifies as "the space of literature."

> In poetry we are no longer referred back to the world, neither to the world as shelter nor to the world as goals. In this language the world recedes and goals cease; the world falls silent; beings with their preoccupations, their projects, their activity are no longer ultimately what speaks ... Then language takes on all of its importance ... It ... speaks as the essential.
>
> (Blanchot 1989: 41)

Language, he recognizes, is far more basic, lasting, essential, and real than are we individual humans who speak and write with it, who use it to express and advance ourselves in the conduct of life. In a deeper sense, language instead uses and outlasts us; it uses us to make its works and enrich its expressive power and influence while negating us as the embodied individuals who own and control those works and their import.

Like the particular person referred to as "this woman," every embodied human being suffers linguistic reduction to a sign, a negating detachment from one's full living presence that Blanchot associates with death, where one's name remains but one's conscious embodied existence is lost. Therefore, "when I say, 'This woman,' real death has been announced and is already present in my language; ... my language essentially signifies the possibility of this destruction" (Blanchot 1995: 323). For Blanchot, this "ideal negation" involved in linguistic reference is a form of "deferred assassination ... Therefore it is accurate to say that when I speak, death speaks in me" (323). The death that linguistic reference implies extends not only to the persons referred to but also to the referring writer. In the space of literature, the writer's reality (and the reader's) is only in the work.

> To say that the poet only exists after the poem means that he receives his "reality" from the poem, but that he does not dispose of this reality except in order to make the poem possible. In this sense he does not survive the creation of the work. He lives by dying in it.
>
> (Blanchot 1989: 227)

As an existential individual in the world, "[the author] is by no means entitled to be cited and glorified by the poem as its origin ... Author and reader are equals with respect to the work and in it ... Neither has any existence except through this work and based upon it" (227).

Blanchot explains the common phenomenon of authors' journals or diaries as a function of the author's anguished death as an individual person in the act of writing. By living "an existence devoted to anguish as the resolution of this [vision of] anguish," by sacrificing oneself to the work, "mak[ing] of things and of himself a burnt offering" to it, the author "proceeds to an existence in which this word *personal* no longer has any meaning" (Blanchot 2001: 44, 132–3). His "recourse to the journal," or personal diary, reminds the author of who he was in the world of things before he died in the space of literature, of "who he is when he isn't writing, when he lives daily life, when he is alive ... not dying" (Blanchot 1989: 29). Paradoxically, however, "the tool he uses in order to recollect himself" to affirm his personal life is precisely what entails his dying self-sacrifice to literature: the act of "writing" (29). Death therefore plays a pervasive, dominant role in Blanchot's fiction and its attempt to communicate a deeper vision of the real.

Literature, he argues, can suggest (though not directly express) a level of reality that is not only beneath and before the world of things and truths that language founds and formulates, but also deeper than language itself, a primordial origin from which language and all existing things and facts emerged. Beneath and before language, there is an "inexpressible reality," where whatever there is remains "incomprehensible because it happens in that anterior region which we cannot designate except under the veil of no" (Blanchot 2001: 138; Blanchot 1989: 222). Lacking language to give it meaning, this deepest reality belongs "to the unnameable, the inhuman, to what is devoid of truth" (Blanchot 1989: 232). We can at best characterize it only in the negative terms of obscurity, darkness, mystery, ambiguity, and emptiness, but great works of literature (or art more generally) can nevertheless direct us toward the experience of this primordial real.

If "the work points us toward the deep of obscurity which we do not think we have designated by calling it elemental," it is not only because of its uncertain, mysterious, enigmatic character in resisting any single, exclusive, incontestable interpretation of meaning (Blanchot 1989: 224). It is also because the work's ambiguities involve an "'exalting alliance of contraries'" that breaks with language's normal constraining logic of individuation, distinction, and contradiction, thus suggesting that "the elemental deep" beneath language is an all-embracing yet irremediably obscure whole (224, 226). Such encompassing wholeness is also an utter emptiness, whose darkness enables the light of language and art to shine forth, whose fluid, shadowy, formlessness allows the forms of objects and events to take shape, whose abyss of untruth and meaninglessness impels us to construct the true and give meaning to our lives. Blanchot describes how art brings us toward "the *original experience*" of this dark abyss of the elemental deep, how "the work draws light from the dark"; how it "revokes the true" to lead us "all the way to the bottom ... [beneath] the domain of truth. The very bottom, the bottomless abyss belongs to art" (237, 239, 241). For "art is that deep which is *sometimes* ... the pure void bereft of importance," yet vitally important in giving us a sense of the primal, grounding space "upon which a foundation can be given," from which language, truth, and significance emerge (239). This is the space of "the intertwining of the Yes and of the No, the ebb and flow of the essential ambiguity" at the deepest level of being, whose dark shadowy presence is absence, but whose absence is equally an enabling presence, because its emptiness is the fullness of the infinite void through which existence arises and in which beings appear and disappear (239).[9]

Literature's essential "emptiness" or "nullity" (epitomized by its fictional detachment from the world of truth) "may constitute an extraordinary force" by suggesting "the obscure depths of existence," the primal void or underlying, all-encompassing space on which language constructs what we call the real world (Blanchot 1995: 301, 343). The work's "realm of the imaginary is not a strange region situated beyond the world, it is the world itself ... as a [vast] whole ... it is the world, grasped and realized in its entirety by the global negation of all the individual realities contained in it, by their disqualification, their absence, by the realization of that absence itself, which is how literary creation begins," that is, from an absence the writer feels compelled both to fill and to express (316). Through this negation, literature suggests the depths of being "before the *world* exists" through language, "of what appears when nothing exists" (328). It further suggests that the origins of language arise from primal nothingness. "Language can begin only with the void; no fullness, no certainty can ever speak ... Negation is tied to language ... Language perceives that its meaning derives not from what exists but from its own retreat before existence" into the symbolic realm (324).

For Blanchot, literature's crucial, irreplaceable role is to remind us of this obscure, primal level of reality, "this anonymous and impersonal flow of being that precedes all [distinct objects of] being," to suggest a sense of "the darkness of existence" (331, 332). Literature can "plunge" us toward "this depth of existence which is neither being nor nothingness" because such existence lies beneath the world of individual beings and even beneath language, whose power of individuation founds those beings (340). Literature evokes these "obscure depths of existence," the void from which the world of things emerges through language, and likewise functions as an "absence by which the thing [as a material object] is annihilated, destroyed in order to become being and idea" through the linguistic sign (343). Just as language creates meaning by negating the concretely living things into signs, so death is the horizon that gives meaning to the individual's life by structuring it within a limited frame of time and space. If the inevitable encompassing nothingness of death is what defines human life, then "we can say that there is being because there is nothingness: death is man's possibility, his chance ... his only hope of being man" (336–7). For Blanchot, language "is *that life which supports death and maintains itself in it* – death, the amazing power of the negative, or freedom, through whose work existence is detached from itself and made significant," emerging, if only briefly, from the enveloping void, the obscure "darkness of existence" (331, 343).

Obscurity and death thus join emptiness and absence, solitude and language as key themes of Blanchot's fiction, pervading even into the titles of his most famous fictional narratives: *Thomas, the Obscure* (1941), *Death Sentence* (1948), and *The Instant of My Death* (1994). The first novella is a love-story wrapped in darkness, impenetrable vagueness, and shadowy ambiguity. Its central event is the death of the female protagonist, and its English text of 117 pages is dominated by words such as "absence," "death," and "night" (appearing, respectively, 63, 68, and 79 times), as well as "nothingness" and "void" (24 and 28 times). The book portrays language as having a life and will of its own, a predatory life that devours Thomas as he reads: "In relation to every symbol, he was in the position of the male praying mantis about to be devoured by the female. They looked at each other ... he perceived all the strangeness there was in being observed by a word as if by a living being ... when the words were already taking hold of him and beginning to read him" while "beginning their carnage" of abstracting live individuals into mere pronouns, "the word *He* and the word *I*" (Blanchot 1988: 25–6).

Like language, thought annihilates the concrete physical person into an idea. Thomas explains:

> It is the property of my thought, not to assure me of existence (as all things do, as a stone does), but to assure me of being in nothingness itself, and to invite me not to be, in order to make me feel my marvellous absence. I think, said Thomas, and this invisible, inexpressible, nonexistent Thomas I became meant that henceforth I was never there where I was ... My existence became entirely that of an absent person who, in every act I performed, produced the same act and did not perform it.
>
> (Blanchot 1988: 99–100)

In being performed in consciousness (in one's mind), the act, to that extent, was not really performed. This suggests that our ordinary living and thinking commit us to continuous dying, by reducing us to a sign through language, to a perceptual image in the gaze of others, or to a mental image even in our own reflective self-consciousness. In contrast, real death brings the relief of being an "eternal dead person" who is free from suffering the objectifying gaze of others and of one's own fatal self-consciousness and who can enjoy death's "immortality in nothingness" (91, 93). Thomas therefore claims, "I had the appearance of any living person, but ... I was real only under the name of death" (92). "I feel myself, living, infinitely more dead than dead. I discover my being in the vertiginous abyss where it is not, an absence, an absence where it sets itself like a god. I am not and I endure," which "causes me to feel, hideously, in a total absence of feeling, my reality in the shape of nothingness" (104).

However, for Blanchot's obscure Thomas, nothingness is the dark, primal, all-encompassing origin of everything. Thomas identifies it with the night, which dissolves the separating contours of things under a blanket of blackness. "Already the void seems to me the ultimate in fullness," the all-enveloping origin of being (103).

> In the night we are inseparable ... The being of a nonbeing of which I am the infinitely small negation...In the night shall I become the universe? ... the origin of that which has no origin...the uncreated is the same word for it and for me ... O night, I am itself.
>
> (106, 108)

The uncreated void and elemental deep, "silence and solitude, were called night ... Absolute night where there were no longer any contradictory terms, where those who suffered were happy, where white found a common substance with black" (76).[10]

In a climactic love scene of *Death Sentence*, Blanchot revisits the notion of an enveloping nocturnal darkness that suggests the mysterious obscurity of primal uncreated reality from which the world emerges through language. Here the narrating protagonist first feels the being of his lover as a vague, shadowy, silent, absent presence in the total darkness of a blackened room at night, before he can touch her or see her or hear her and before even knowing who she is.

> Blackest space extended before me. I was not in this blackness, but at the edge of it, and I confess that it is terrifying. It is terrifying because there is something in it which scorns man and which man cannot endure without losing himself. But he must lose himself; and whoever resists will founder, and whoever goes forward will become this very blackness, this cold and dead and scornful thing in the very heart of which lives the infinite.
>
> (Blanchot 1978: 67–8)

Blanchot's writing impels us to face "the depths of the horrible," impersonal primal reality with its unending, uncaring cycle of life and death upon which we, through language, construct our world of persons, things, and feelings (68). This world includes, of course, the aesthetic objects and feelings that we encounter in literary works, whose authors struggle to create their radiant, well-wrought forms from such discomforting visions of reality's horrible, dark underside.

Eliot: Extending Human Consciousness to Convey Wisdom and the Inexpressible

Like Bataille and Blanchot, T.S. Eliot probed the ghastly grim depths of reality with brave persistence. Perhaps life's horrors were painfully evident to their generation that suffered two devastating world wars, bloody revolutions, and the holocaust. In any case, the dark realities of death, nothingness, loneliness, devastation, and lack of meaning permeate Eliot's verse. Like his admired John Webster and John Donne, Eliot "was much possessed by death / And saw the skull beneath the skin" and "knew the anguish of the marrow / The ague of the skeleton" (Eliot 1969: 52 [lines 1–2, 13–14]). The title of his most famous poem, *The Waste Land*, along with two of its section titles ("The Burial of the Dead" and "Death by Water") highlight the themes of death and barren nothingness that resonate throughout the work, suggesting the essential continuity or fusion of life and death that makes one's living state a state of dying, one's being a meaningless nothing. "I was neither / Living nor dead, and I knew nothing ... A crowd flowed over London Bridge, so many, / I had not thought death had undone so many ... 'That corpse you planted last year in your garden, / 'Has it begun to sprout? Will it bloom this year?" (Eliot 1969: 62–3 [lines 39–40, 62–3, 71–2]). "Nothing again nothing ... 'You know nothing? Do you see nothing? Do you remember nothing?'... 'Are you alive, or not? Is there nothing in your head?'" (65 [lines 120–3, 126]). "I can connect / Nothing with nothing" (70 [lines 301–2]). "He who was living is now dead / We who were living are now dying / With a little patience" (72 [lines 328–30]).

"The Hollow Men" depicts a similar world of gloomy emptiness and death. "This is the dead land" in "this valley of dying stars" where "Our dried voices ... Are quiet and meaningless" in "death's twilight kingdom / The hope only / Of empty men ... This is the way the world ends / Not with a bang but a whimper" (83–6 [lines 5, 7, 39, 54, 65–7, 97–8]). If Eliot's lifelessly timid Alfred J. Prufrock declares "'I am Lazarus, come from the dead, / Come back to tell you all'... [but] It is impossible to say just what I mean!" (16 [lines 95–6, 106]), the brutish protagonist of *Sweeney Agonistes* baldly affirms the identity of life and death while gesturing towards a more fundamental reality beneath the level of language and meaning, and devoid of any sense of cultural refinement that language and meaning might bring. Reality is the brute, repetitive, endless, and meaningless biological cycle of birth, reproduction, and death. "Birth, and copulation, and death. / That's all the facts when you come to brass tacks ... Life is death" (122, 124). This deeper level of existence that we share with lower animals, this surging cyclical stream of life beneath language's differentiation of beings and meanings where opposites like death and life merge in an endless senseless flow, is impossible to capture in words, as Sweeney admits. But words are all we have. "Death is life and life is death / I gotta use words when I talk to you / But if you understand or if you don't / That's nothing to me and nothing to you" (125). For *nothing* is ultimately *all* we can meaningfully understand in the absurdly "perpetual recurrence of ... birth and dying! / The endless cycle" of life that always "brings us nearer to death" but "no nearer to God," who provides the key to redeeming the meaningless wasteland of our mortal existence (147).

These dark themes (and the answering hope of divine salvation) resound, expand, and deepen in Eliot's culminating poetic masterpiece, *Four Quartets*, which gives his ultimate vision of reality a different tonality than Bataille's and Blanchot's. Here the world's senseless cycle of death and destitution is tempered by the redemptive promise of the godly otherworld. The first poem, "Burnt Norton," avows that "human kind / Cannot bear very much reality," and then reveals a metaphysical vision of an all-encompassing, distinction-defying totality that dissolves everything, even the divisions of time, into an eternal, comprehensive present, "the still point of the turning world" that is "neither arrest nor movement" (172–3).

> Time past and time future
> What might have been and what has been
> Point to one end, which is always present.
> ...
> At the still point of the turning world. Neither flesh nor fleshless;
> Neither from nor towards; at the still point, there the dance is,
> But neither arrest nor movement.
>
> (172–3)

The poem urges to go deeper into this baffling world where the differential logic of language and meaning disintegrates into a dark, lonely, senseless void.

> Descend lower, descend only
> Into the world of perpetual solitude,
> World not world, but that which is not world,
> Internal darkness, deprivation
> And destitution of all property,
> Desiccation of the world of sense,
> Evacuation of the world of fancy,
> Inoperancy of the world of spirit;
> ...
>
> Words move, music moves
> Only in time; but that which is only living
> Can only die. Words, after speech, reach
> Into the silence.
>
> (174–5)

And we who live only (and but briefly) in time are, like words, invariably "Caught in the form of limitation / Between un-being and being," and unable to fathom the meaning of life that leads us all to the darkness and silence of death (175). As "East Coker" puts it: "O dark dark dark. They all go into the dark / The vacant interstellar spaces, the vacant into the vacant," reenacting a baffling, ever-repeating, "echoed ecstasy / Not lost, but requiring, pointing to the agony / Of death and birth," whose existential, felt experience lies ineffably beneath language and meaning (180), and beyond the life of any individual. "We had the experience but missed the meaning," which "Is not the experience of one life only / But of many generations—not forgetting / Something that is probably quite ineffable: / The backward look ... towards the primitive terror" (186–7).

This primal experience of fundamental reality and its never-ending flux of mortal life (where "the time of death is every moment") is something death can express better than discourse (188). "And what the dead had no speech for, when living, / They can tell you, being dead: the communication / Of the dead is tongued with fire beyond the language of the living" (192). Language imposes a determinate structure on primal experience to generate meaning and knowledge, but by doing so it falsifies our experience of the elemental real, which is immediate, indeterminate, ineffable, changing, and flowing. "The knowledge imposes a pattern, and falsifies, / For the pattern is new in every moment ... and shocking" (179). Every effort "to use words ... / Is ... a different kind of failure ... a raid on the inarticulate / With shabby equipment always deteriorating" (182). As words cannot truly capture the meaning of lived experience and knowledge of primal reality, "The only wisdom we can hope to acquire / Is the wisdom of humility: humility is endless" (179). Although words are inadequate to convey the depths of experience and primal reality's all-embracing whole that dissolves distinctions and merges opposites (past and future, fixity and flux, beginning and end, up and down), Eliot argues that literature (especially poetry) provides the best way for language to approach this dark, inexpressible, difference-defying whole and to communicate wisdom.

Before examining his arguments for this in his prose theorizing, let me suggest how poetry's power to express unity that overrides difference depends not only on its abandoning the constraining logic of practical discourse and thus suspending disbelief, but also on its ontological complexity. First, poetry unites contradictories by harmoniously combining their words on the same lines with a unifying, satisfying rhythm that dispels the discord of obvious contraries or contradictions. Consider Eliot's lines: "World not world, but that which is not world"; "Death is life and life is death"; "And the fire and the rose are one" (125, 174, 198). The materiality of these contrasting words, their physical co-presence in the same line, and their sonic unity in being each only one syllable all serve to diminish their opposition through a repetitive, unifying rhythm and shared visual line. Second, poetry unites two modes of being, existing as oral performance that moves in time (where uttered words appear then disappear) but also as written or printed text where all the words are simultaneously present on the page, where they manifest their being in time past, time present, and time future. As both enduring textual object and temporal sonic event, with all their multiple sensory properties and ideal meanings, a poem embraces the opposites of fixity and flux, materiality and ideality, and thus serves (with its signature figure of metaphor) as an emblem for the unification of contrasts through an aesthetic of *discordia concours*.[11]

Eliot's modernism is distinctive in emphasizing the ancient philosophical ideal of wisdom and maintaining that literature can best convey it. Wisdom differs from knowledge because it requires a dimension of moral virtue and resists reduction to discursive truth. It finds expression in silence and the humility of cognitive fallibilism, an admission to knowing next to nothing with certainty. "Where is the wisdom we have lost in knowledge? / Where is the knowledge we have lost in information?" Eliot asks in "The Rock" (147). Though wisely eschewing to define wisdom ("There is no word, however, more impossible to define, and no word more difficult to understand"), Eliot describes it as a "gift of intuition, ripened and given application by experience, for understanding the nature of things, certainly of living things, most certainly of the human heart" (Eliot 1957: 220–1). The wise person must have "a very wide range of interest, sympathy and understanding" held together by some "fundamental Unity" expressing an insightful vision of "Life itself, the World seen from a particular point of view" based on intelligence and experience (Eliot 1957: 214). Wisdom means not only having a coherent vision of the world but also recognizing it as fallible and limited, as only one possible point of view; it thus requires a fallibilist humility with flexible openness for accommodating new experience and a tolerant recognition that there are other reasonable world-views. In short, it requires "the charity that comes from understanding human beings in all their variety ... [and] ... diverse beliefs" and must be something more and other than a "sum of wise sayings" or philosophical truths (Eliot 1957: 221). Hence "Philosophy without wisdom is vain" and "unbalanced," and we should make "a distinction between the *philosophy* of a poet and his *wisdom*" (Eliot 1976a: 67; Eliot 1957: 224).

Literature, Eliot believes, is the most effective way for language to convey wisdom. This is because properly appreciating great literature involves imaginatively understanding a wide variety of alien worlds of experience and belief, each reflecting a coherent perception of life, which can help us test and develop our own beliefs and vision of the world. Literature inculcates the charitable appreciation of different points of view, through the edification and the amusement they afford us in the aesthetically appealing forms of expression that literature gives them. Great literature, moreover, communicates not only a perception of meaningful order in life but also a powerful sense of life's unfathomable mystery; and our efforts to understand authors of genius bring us greater awareness of our own inadequacies and limitation. Here, surely, great literature teaches the wisdom of humility.

Literature best conveys wisdom because it works by indirection (by evoking, comparing, and refining attitudes, insights, and feelings) rather than by directly formulated doctrines.

> For wisdom is communicated on a deeper level than that of logical propositions; all language is inadequate, but probably the language of poetry is the language most capable of communicating wisdom. The wisdom of a great poet is concealed in his work; but in becoming aware of it we become ourselves more wise.
>
> (Eliot 1957: 226)

This play of concealment and awareness shapes literature's indirect mode of edification. It does not lead to wisdom by direct preaching, by formulating maxims or rules for being wise. Instead, literature instructs through pleasure, by entertaining us with interesting ideas that stimulate and enrich our imagination and critical thought, thus augmenting our resources for wisdom. Eliot therefore strikingly defines poetry in terms of pleasure, entertainment, and amusement. Affirming that the poet "would like to be something of a popular entertainer, and ... would like to convey the pleasures of poetry" (Eliot 1964b: 154), Eliot claims that "poetry is a superior amusement" that "has something to give us besides pleasure: for if it were only pleasure, the pleasure itself could not be of the highest kind" (Eliot 1976b: viii; Eliot 1957: 18). In good poetry the pleasure always involves "the communication of some new experience, or some fresh understanding of the familiar, or the expression of something we have experienced but have no words for, which enlarges our consciousness or refines our sensibility" (Eliot 1957: 18). But as "the meaning of a poem exists in the words of the poem and in those words only," so "the wisdom of poetry ... would not be communicated at all, if it were not experienced by the reader as poetry" (Eliot 1957: 222, 225).

Although "the wisdom and the poetry are inseparable," we cannot directly obtain this wisdom in the pleasure of reading a poem or any literary work. In this sense, the wisdom of literature lies concealed beneath its surface and is communicated indirectly through a two-stage process of reading (Eliot 1957: 226).

> It is simply not true that works of fiction, prose or verse ... *directly* extend our knowledge of life. Direct knowledge of life is knowledge directly in relation to ourselves [from personal experience] ... Knowledge of life obtained through fiction is only possible by another stage of self-consciousness.
>
> (Eliot 1976c: 395)

After having pleasurably immersed ourselves in the words, ideas, and values of our reading, we must step back and assess them in terms of our own experience and critical intelligence, so "we can see, and allow for, their differences from ourselves" (Eliot 1976c: 396). Great literature can make us wiser not by directly instilling particular formulas for wisdom but "because in the process of being affected by [the different visions of their authors] ... we cease to be dominated by any one [vision] ... The very different views of life, cohabiting in our minds, affect each other, and our own personality asserts itself" to form our own perspective on life, while tempering it with the wisdom of fallibilist pluralism, that every point of view has limitations and blind spots, including our own (Eliot 1976c: 395).

The very notion of point of view, which Eliot's Bradleyan doctoral thesis defined in terms of "finite centres," implies such limitation and the existence of other, different points of view on life that even the same individual comes to occupy in the changing stream of her experience (Eliot 1964a: 147). There is thus no guarantee that one's experience or feelings will be understood by others or even by one's subsequent self. Communication of one's inner life is always a courageous act of faith across a gulf of privacy and difference; and "the life of a soul does not consist in the contemplation of one consistent world but in the painful task of unifying (to a greater or less extent) jarring and incompatible ones" (147).

Language, therefore, is the instrument that enables this bridging or sharing of our inevitably divergent inner experiences, and Eliot insists that the poet's prime social function is to serve language and its powers for sharing by making it more effective in communication. This does not mean reducing language to bare practical functionality through the homogeneity of the simplest forms of expression. Rather, poetry serves to "preserve, and even restore, the beauty of a language," while updating it with new words and metaphors "for the changing purposes of modern life," thus "contributing to the development and maintaining the quality, the capacity of the language to express a wide range, and subtle gradation, of feeling and emotion" (Eliot 1957: 22–3, 37–8). The poet develops language through "an attempt to extend the confines of the human consciousness and to report of things unknown, to express the inexpressible" (Eliot 1957: 169). Invested with "the obligation to explore, to find words for the inarticulate, to capture those feelings which people can hardly even feel, because they have no words for them," the poet must also remember "that the explorer beyond the frontiers of ordinary consciousness will only be able to return and report to his fellow-citizens," if he does not lose touch with their realities and language (Eliot 1978: 134). This is why Eliot so often insists "that poetry must not stray too far from the ordinary everyday language which we use and hear" (Eliot 1957: 29). It is also why he insists that the great poet as "master of a language should be the great servant of it," even to the point of sacrificing oneself and one's personal feelings (Eliot 1978: 133).

This of course recalls Eliot's famous "Impersonal theory of poetry," that good poetry is not the expression of the poet's actual psychological sentiments as a particular personality but rather the sacrifice or extinction of that personality for the sake and service of poetry and language in expressing feelings that are somehow new or special but as yet inarticulate. "The progress of an artist is a continual self-sacrifice, a continual extinction of personality," similar in thrust to Blanchot's notion that literature annihilates the author as person (Eliot 1976c: 17). "The poet's mind is in fact a receptacle for seizing and storing up numberless feelings, phrases, images ... which can unite to form a new compound" (Eliot 1976c: 19). Rather than deriving from a distinct feeling or idea that the poet seeks to express with deliberate premeditation, poetry begins with an "obscure impulse" that emerges from some deeper realm of experienced reality and seizes the poet who is thus involuntarily possessed,

> oppressed by a burden which he must bring to birth in order to obtain relief. Or, to change the figure of speech, he is haunted by a demon, a demon against which he feels powerless, because in its first manifestation it has no face, no name, nothing; and the words, the poem he makes, are a kind of form of exorcism of this demon.
>
> (Eliot 1957: 98)

If poetry arises from a troubling, obscurely demonic possession emerging from the inarticulate dark depths of a reality beneath language but requiring language for its exorcism, then Eliot presents another way of understanding Bataille's linking of literature and "*le mal*" (whose French meaning includes not only "evil" but more generally all sorts of bad or troubling things). Through our experiences of life and our reading of literature we sometimes catch a haunting glimpse of a brutal, painful, formless, primitive reality beneath the level of language and meaning; but we can study this horrific, inarticulate vision only by trying to render it somehow in language. Moreover, the best way we can bear this anguished vision of horror and most effectively communicate it to others is through the alluring, entertaining power of literature.

Russell: Skepticism So Darkly Radical That It Requires Fiction

Bertrand Russell, whose public personality and literary products were utterly unlike Bataille's, Blanchot's, and Eliot's, also differed from them in writing an autobiography. He prefaced it, however, with two short texts expressing an existential vision surprisingly similar to theirs: a life suffused with the intertwining passions of ecstasy and anguish, of frenzied madness and the painful gloom of loneliness. The book's (handwritten) verse dedication to his fourth wife Edith begins: "Through the long years I sought peace. / I found ecstasy, I found anguish, I found madness, / I found loneliness. / I found the solitary pain that gnaws the heart, / But peace I did not find" (Russell 1975: v). Then, in a prologue ("What I Have Lived for"), Russell reveals:

> Three passions, simple but overwhelmingly strong, have governed my life: the longing for love, the search for knowledge, and unbearable pity for the suffering of mankind. These passions, like great winds, have blown me hither and thither, in a wayward course, over a deep ocean of anguish, reaching to the very verge of despair.
>
> (9)

Russell explains that he "sought love, first, because it brings ecstasy" but also "because it relieves loneliness" and suggests through its blissful union "a mystic miniature" of the heavenly existence described by "saints and poets," thus providing salutary respite from his hauntingly grim vision of reality as a "cold unfathomable lifeless abyss" ruled by senseless confusion, contingency, and death (9).[12]

Russell's most famous essay, "A Free Man's Worship," describes us humans as "puppets" in an uncaring universe of "irresistible forces ... – Death and change" and endless strife; it insists "that all is passing in this mad, monstrous world, that all is struggling to snatch, at any cost, a few brief moments of life before Death's inexorable decree" (Russell 1953a: 50, 57). Not only do "the silent orders of omnipotent Death" obliterate our human lives and those of all other creatures but they will destroy everything meaningful we have created, even the entire world itself through "the vast death of the solar system," where all human achievement "must inevitably be buried beneath the debris of a universe of ruins" (51, 59). Although it is horribly depressing to face this "hostile universe" that cares nothing for human life or meaning and has "evil always in view," it is intellectually irresponsible, Russell argues, to make a religious leap of faith and wishfully suppose that an omnipotent, loving God has wisely orchestrated this universal "tyranny of death" for our ultimate salvation (53, 54). Instead, we must courageously address reality's horrors with the Stoic "virtue of resignation" and the "submission of our desires, but not of our thoughts" to the limits of an uncaring universe (54). "But passive renunciation is not the whole of wisdom"; for despite our "powerlessness ... before the blind hurry of the universe," we can maintain our "knowledge of good and evil" and "the freedom of our thoughts [from which] springs the whole world of art and philosophy, and the vision of beauty" (53, 54, 55, 58). Although reality's "sure doom falls pitiless and dark" upon us, we can take comfort and "worship at the shrine that [our] own hands have built; undismayed by the empire of chance, to preserve a mind free" to contemplate and "sustain ... the world that [our] own ideals have fashioned despite the trampling march of unconscious power" (59).

Although devoting so much of his life to the search for knowledge, Russell grew progressively dubious of what we claim to know and of the value of our knowledge. Dubbed by one biographer, "the passionate sceptic," Russell came to emphasize, like Eliot, the crucial importance of wisdom as a superior and necessary guide for knowledge.[13] "With every increase of knowledge and skill, wisdom becomes more necessary, for every such increase augments our capacity for realizing our purposes, and therefore augments our capacity for evil, if our purposes are unwise" (Russell 1956: 177). For Russell, as for Eliot, wisdom requires a "comprehensive vision" that includes "not only intellect but also feeling" and a moral dimension of "emancipation" from "egoism" and "narrow-mindedness" toward greater "impartiality" (174–5, 177). This enables us to contemplate with understanding the differing ideas and practices of people existing "remote in time or space" from us while also "giving to such things their due weight in our feelings" (175).[14] If "philosophic contemplation" promotes wisdom's emancipatory "enlargement of the Self" by "suggest[ing] many possibilities which enlarge our thoughts and free them from the tyranny of custom" and "enrich our intellectual imagination" while diminishing "arrogant dogmatism," then so should the very divergent visions of life we find in fictional literature, which appeal both to our minds and our feelings (Russell 1959: 91–3).

Russell's turn to fiction reflects this conclusion. The question remains, however, what, if anything, makes fiction superior to philosophy in communicating wisdom? If philosophy provides ample materials for wisdom, and if Russell's own philosophical prose is evidently clear in conveying the dismal vision that reality at bottom is dark, uncaring, violent, chaotic, senseless, evil, and pervaded with the doom of death,[15] then what advantage does literature have over philosophy and ordinary discourse? Russell's fiction suggests an answer that he never articulates in his philosophical writings. The answer is that fiction is better for communicating the wisdom of skepticism, because its non-assertive discourse eschews commitment to the truth of its propositions and thereby enables them to convey radical skeptical ideas without falling into the self-contradiction of claiming them true.

Russell does not articulate this point in introducing his stories and describing their purpose. Instead, he insists that he wrote them purely for his own "pleasure" and that of prospective readers, claiming he "should be very sorry if it were supposed that the stories are meant to point a moral or illustrate a doctrine. Each of them was written for its own sake, simply as a story, and if it is found interesting or amusing it has served its purpose" (Russell 1953b: vii–viii). Russell later confessed other motivations, both psychological and cognitive.

> The writing of these stories was a great release of my hitherto unexpressed feelings and of thoughts which could not be stated without mention of fears that had no rational basis ... I could state in fiction ideas which I half believed in but had no good solid grounds for believing. In this way it was possible to warn of dangers which might or might not occur in the near future.
>
> (Russell 1975: 525)

Russell further claimed to have "often found fables the best way of making a point" (Russell 1975: 527), but he never asserted the particular power of fiction in communicating philosophical theses like radical skepticism that seem too paradoxical for straightforward assertion. I believe, however, that he suggests this idea most clearly in his fiction, and we can demonstrate its role in the first three short stories from Russell's *Satan in the Suburbs*. To do so requires plot summaries.

1. The book's first story "Satan in the Suburbs, or Horrors Manufactured Here" is a first-person narrative whose scientist narrator strives to resolve a mysterious advertisement posted on a neighboring suburban villa: "Horrors manufactured here. Apply Dr. Murdoch Mallako" (Russell 1953b: 1). The mystery becomes more sinister when four of the narrator's respectable neighbors undergo horrible misfortune after visiting Mallako. Through various efforts the narrator learns what happened in these visits. In each case, curiosity brought the victim to Mallako, who seemed able to read the victim's hidden desires and who told each victim a tale of someone in extremely similar conditions who was able to satisfy the same desires through a clever but grossly immoral course of action. Each neighbor-victim acts according to the relevant model but with ruinous results, and the narrator is unable to help them. Sickened by Mallako's wickedness and his neighbors' moral weaknesses that together reveal the hideous horrors of human iniquity, the narrator plans to cleanse the world of sin and frustrate Mallako's evil doings by creating a machine that will destroy all life on earth. However, when Mallako discovers the plan and supports it, explaining his total hatred of the human race, the narrator changes his mind and kills only Mallako, framing the shooting as a suicide. Though the murder goes undetected, the narrator remains haunted by the idea that Mallako and evil still triumph through the very crime the narrator committed. His subsequent confession of the murder is taken for insanity, and he is consigned to a madhouse.

2. "The Corsican Ordeal of Miss X" (which Russell earlier published anonymously) is also narrated in the first person. The narrator is a friend and colleague of Professor N, an expert in pre-Celtic decorative art, whose secretary, Miss X, has recently returned from a holiday in the island of Corsica mysteriously distraught and depressed. Neither Professor N nor the narrator is able to extract any information from Miss X about what troubles her, and the narrator resolves to uncover the mystery so that something could be done to aid her. He begins by consulting a local acquaintance of Corsican descent who evasively sends him to a supporter of the Corsican nationalist cause. Feigning Corsican patriotism, the narrator obtains a letter of introduction to the Corsican activist Count Aspromante and travels to the island to meet him. The Count then takes the narrator on a very arduous journey to the Count's mountain castle. There the narrator is introduced to the (disguised) leader of the Corsican cause, who agrees to solve the mystery by giving the narrator a sealed note for Miss X declaring that she is released from her oath of silence. The narrator hurriedly returns to England and presents the note to Miss X in Professor N's office. Miss X laments that the note may solve the mystery but not her sorrow, and then sadly relates her tale. During her Corsican visit, she saw the Count's mountain castle,

which aroused her curiosity. Exploring it, she discovered by chance a meeting of Corsican activists and overheard their plot to kill various heads of state and also her beloved Professor N (because of his "traitorous theories" that pre-Celtic decorative art came from Lithuania, not Corsica). Shocked by the threat to her beloved boss, Miss X emitted a cry and was captured. Under threat of torture, she vowed to undergo the ordeal of keeping silent about the plot and performing herself the murder of Professor N. Though now released from silence, she remains bound by her oath to kill. However, Professor N kindly resolves to do the one thing that can free her from this remaining oath – the impossibility of killing a dead man. He therefore kills himself on the spot, and she is so moved that she follows suit. The narrator's feelings of guilt tempt him to do likewise, but he instead leaves to inform the police and frustrate the Corsican plot of political assassinations.

3. "The Infra-redioscope" relates an ingenious plot for world domination, conceived and executed by four magnates in the powers of finance, advertising, science, and the press. The plot involves fabricating a scientifically complex but totally phony machine – the infra-redioscope – that allegedly reveals the invisible through infrared photography. The plotters use the instrument to claim the fake news of the sighting of strange invisible creatures, later alleged to be invaders from Mars. The appearance of these creatures is designed, painted, and first reported by Lady Millicent, the beautiful young wife of the financier, who thus becomes party to the fraud. Initial public skepticism is overcome by the strength of the four scheming powers who dominate public opinion and can stifle dissent. Moreover, the anti-Martian panic that ensues has marvelous effects, uniting East and West against a common foe and thus establishing world peace. However, a young, dedicated scientist remains unconvinced by the story and confronts Lady Millicent to learn the truth. She confesses to him, but he falls in love with her and is torn between allegiance to the truth and, on the other hand, his concern for the welfare of Millicent and world peace; both would be ruined by exposure of the fraud. Unable to decide his course of action, he kills himself; and Millicent is so moved that she publicly confesses. The resulting end of Martian terror unhappily permits a recrudescence of East-West dissension that soon develops into full-scale war. However, suddenly all armies and civilian populations fall dead. The Martians have invaded!

***

Russell's stories obviously encourage philosophical interpretation. As he remarks in his preface, "the stories are not intended to be realistic" (Russell 1953b: vii). Their obvious lack of realism and their preoccupation with ethical dilemmas (truth versus love, pleasure versus virtue, and conflicts of duties such as promise-keeping versus not inflicting harm) suggest the symbolic meaning of parables. The stories' mannered, slightly stilted style (with remarks such as "Let the cleansing fire of truth purge your soul of dross") creates the sermonizing tone of an exemplum; and Russell's use of proper names is particularly suggestive of allegory (Russell 1953b: 109). Designating characters as Miss X and Professor N, whose initials are among the most universal of mathematical symbols, implies that they have an essentially symbolic role. The names and order of Mallako's victims likewise suggest their symbolic role as exempla: Abercrombie, Beauchamp, Cartwright, and Ellerker are victims A, B, C, and E (and the absence of victim D will serve to make a skeptical point). Other names in the stories suggest symbolic interpretation not by analogy to mathematical variables but by their own connotations: Doctor Mallako, purveyor of evil (*le mal*) and a Machiavellian variation of the devilish, man-devouring Molloch; Sir Publius Harper, the magnate of advertising; the wealthy Lady Millicent; and the penurious, skeptical scientist who loved her, (doubting) Thomas Shovelpenny. Moreover, all the three stories (indeed all five of the collection) are structured on epistemological themes: the search for knowledge, the resolution of mystery, and the problem of appearance versus reality. As epistemological exempla inculcating the vanity of human knowledge, the stories combine to present a skepticism more radical than that of Russell's nonfictional writings.

This radical skeptical position includes three main ideas. First, the desire for knowledge is extremely dangerous and can lead to disaster. Second, human knowledge is meagre, fallible, and extremely difficult to attain. Third, truth and knowledge, even if attained, are not essentially helpful and can do more harm than good. Together these ideas portray a dismal view of human knowledge. Not only is it unsafe to seek the truth, but, if we seek it, we are not likely to find it; and even if we find it, it will do us no good. Each of the stories reveals the dangers and disasters that result from curiosity's desire for knowledge. Miss X suffers her horrible ordeal and ultimate suicide because of her curiosity to learn more about the mountain castle. She herself bewails the moral: "Curiosity, that fatal passion which misled our first mother, lured me on" (Russell 1953b: 78). Though Miss X is clearly the story's main example of the dangers of the inquiring mind, Professor N is also condemned to death by his search for knowledge, despite its being in the apparently innocuous field of pre-Celtic decorative art. The narrator, who too seeks knowledge to resolve the mystery but manages to survive, appears to be a counterexample. But we can explain his survival as formally necessary for the narration and for the frustration of the Corsican plot. One could also interpret it as symbolizing the belief that only the purely detached inquirer, who is not personally involved or affected by the matter investigated, is protected from the hazards of the search for truth. In other words, the scientist or scholar is safe only when his study is wholly detached and impersonal.

However, the stories show this strategy for safe inquiry is ultimately not viable, because our affective human nature cannot remain wholly detached and personally uninvolved in the quest for truth, particularly as the knowledge we seek seems inevitably to concern or affect one's fellow humans and oneself. Thus, in "Satan in the Suburbs," after the victims and the narrator are initially led into Mallako's clutches by curiosity, the narrator tries to banish Mallako from his mind by concentrating on his own scientific research. However, knowledge of his neighbors' misfortunes compels the narrator to abandon disinterested research in order to take up the struggle against Mallako, which inevitably leads to his own downfall. Similarly, in "The Infra-Redioscope," the young scientist survives as long as his inquiry is detached and impersonal; but once he becomes personally and emotionally involved by falling in love with the beautiful Millicent, he is led to suicide. He unprofitably chides himself, "'Come, come' ... 'you are not here to feel emotions. You are here to conduct a grave investigation'" (Russell 1953b: 108). The obvious moral is that we humans simply cannot remain wholly disinterested in the search for truth; our emotions are naturally engaged and cannot be successfully suppressed, because affect is even necessary to stimulate and sustain inquiry.

The stories also demonstrate, in different ways, the second skeptical thesis – the difficulty and fallibility of human knowledge. "The Corsican Ordeal of Miss X" exemplifies it symbolically through the extensive, arduous research the narrator must make to uncover the secret, efforts partly symbolized by the strenuous mountain journey. Moreover, the tales give striking examples of human complicity to conceal or suppress the truth. Besides the Corsican oath of silence, there is the secret plot of Millicent's husband and his associates, which received the silent complicity of knowing scientists who were convinced that the fraud served world peace and that keeping quiet about it also served their own personal interests. In "Satan in the Suburbs," we see the refusal of Ministry officials to tolerate the propagation of a truth because it would inexpediently threaten a valued researcher who, with Mallako's aid, seduced and ruined Mrs. Ellerker and caused the death of her husband and an innocent aviator. The fallibility of human knowledge finds further expression through fundamental logical fallacies that function prominently in the stories. For instance, the ruin of all the narrator's neighbors in "Satan in the Suburbs" is based on their overly hasty acceptance of the argument from analogy. Mallako tells them case histories of people with circumstances and desires almost identical to their own and who obtain their desires through certain risky actions. Each victim generalizes from the single case analogous to his or her own, and they all infer that because the circumstances are so similar, analogous action on their part will yield similarly successful results. But the results prove disastrous. Thus, the Humean "animal faith" in induction (the belief that what has been will be, that similar antecedents will have similar results) which is the cornerstone of human knowledge, leads each neighbor to ruination. This story also highlights the fallibility of induction and hasty generalization in a formalistic way by means of the names and order of the victims. The first, Mr. Abercrombie (victim A), is followed by Mr. Beauchamp and Mr. Cartwright (victims B and C). The natural inference is that the pattern will be continued by a fourth male victim whose name begins with a "D," but this induction is quickly shown wrong on both counts. The fourth victim is a Mrs. Ellerker ("a lurker"?), as if to suggest that error is always lurking behind induction, if not behind all human belief.

"The Infra-Redioscope" highlights another logical fallacy, the *Fallacy of Denying the Antecedent*, which can be formally represented by the invalid inference: $(p \rightarrow q), \neg p \therefore \neg q$. It states that given the truth of the conditional "if p then q," although the truth of the antecedent (p) entails the truth of the consequent (q), the falsity of the antecedent ($\neg p$) does *not* entail the falsity of the consequent ($\neg q$) . For example, though it is valid to argue that if Jones is a Roman Catholic, then he is a Christian, it is not valid to infer that if Jones is not a Roman Catholic, then he is not a Christian. In "The Infra-redioscope" the fallacy is manifested thus: if Millicent and company are telling the truth (p), then there exist Martians who threaten to invade earth (q). But because they are found to be lying ($\neg p$), it is inferred by all the world that there are no such Martians ($\neg q$). This formally invalid but seemingly reasonable inference is soon revealed as disastrously fallacious. Martians invade an unprepared and war-ridden earth and destroy humankind. Human knowledge and reasoning have failed again, and at what a price! The fallacy-exposing Martian invasion is particularly powerful in its skeptical impact, because it not only stuns the people in the story, who are convinced that they now know the truth about the Martian fraud. It also astounds us readers, who are equally smug in the "knowledge" that the Martian invasion is a horrible hoax that could not possibly be true. The intended effect of this surprise ending is to shock us into recognizing how little we know, how easily we err, and how our alleged certainties are not really certain.

The stories' third skeptical thesis maintains that knowledge, even when attained, is not necessarily beneficial. Knowledge can be as much an evil as a good, and, at least for the purposes of human life, a lie can be more beneficial than the truth. The narrator of "Satan in the Suburbs" learns of Mallako's evil doings, but this knowledge does not help him save the victims, as Mallako scornfully reminds him. The Ministry officials whom the narrator approaches to seek Mrs. Ellerker's release and have her seducer punished are not interested in the truth because it is inexpedient. Nor is anyone interested in knowing about his murdering Mallako. Indeed, insistence on this truth only results in his being sent to a madhouse. "The Corsican Ordeal of Miss X" similarly exemplifies the uselessness of knowledge, as the narrator solves the mystery of Miss X's depression, but this knowledge can neither remedy her misery nor save her beloved Professor N from sudden death. She herself complains that though knowledge may "lift the veil of mystery," "it will not remove the cause of sorrow" (Russell 1953b: 77); and we should recall that it is their knowledge that kills them both.

"The Infra-redioscope" shows how belief in a tissue of lies (namely, that the infra-redioscope could and did reveal invisible creatures who were the advance guard of invading Martians) can promote tremendous human good – establishing world peace and unity in the face of a common threat. In contrast, the knowledge of the hoax brings the evils of dissension and world war, which (the story suggests), encourage the Martian invasion that destroys all humankind. As the world in general thrives on lies and suffers from truth, so does the individual – even the scientist or truth-seeker. The hard-earned knowledge that the infra-redioscope was a fraud only brings the young scientist misery and death. Through the mouth of this dedicated but doomed scientist, Russell seems to voice his own grave doubts on the value of human knowledge:

> perhaps it is only through lies that men can be induced to live sensibly. Perhaps human passions are such that to the end of time truth will be dangerous. Perhaps I have erred in giving my allegiance to truth ... When I was a younger man I had hopes, high hopes. I thought that I should be able to dedicate my life to the twin gods of truth and humanity ... Nay, it is impossible ... But as I die I leave to my successors this dreadful choice – the choice between truth and life.
>
> (Russell 1953b: 112–14)

Here truth appears as not only valueless to life but indeed starkly opposed to it, so that one must choose between them. Millicent ultimately chooses truth, and the consequence is the destruction of humanity. In suggesting the moral that we should abandon truth in order to live, Russell's story presents a shocking view for a philosopher who devoted a lifetime to the quest for knowledge.

How, then, should we interpret the radical skepticism expressed in Russell's fiction? If his philosophical writings had a skeptical spirit, they never so thoroughly doubted the value of truth and science. Contrasting science to philosophy in terms of what we "know and ... do not know," Russell, in his nonfictional writing, continued to urge the cognitive message of "A Free Man's Worship," insisting on the courageous, impartial pursuit of knowledge and the Stoic acceptance of that knowledge, cruel though it be (Russell 1972: 141). "It is not by delusion, however exalted, that mankind can prosper but only by unswerving courage in the pursuit of truth," he wrote in a late essay (Russell 1962b: 48). Yet it is hard not to take Russell's fictional voicing of skepticism as expressing his own deep doubts. He seems to identify himself so closely with the despairing views of the young scientist Shovelpenny that he inappropriately speaks through him. Shovelpenny's lament "When I was a younger man I had hopes, high hopes" is not a fitting remark for the young man he is in the story, but it is very appropriate for an old man like Russell (Russell 1953b: 113).

Why, then, did Russell confine his extreme skepticism to fiction and not assert its radical views more directly in his philosophical prose? If we discount timidity and shame (as we certainly should, given Russell's indisputable boldness), then one likely explanation is fiction's special capacity for avoiding entanglement in the ancient trap for radical skeptics. This is the performative self-contradiction that in asserting such skepticism we are affirming our global ignorance yet simultaneously claiming to know something true. Ancient skeptics like Sextus Empiricus tried to deal with this problem by explaining away skeptical assertions as mere reports of momentary feelings or as hypotheses that were entertained (as Montaigne put it) "without adherence or consent" (Montaigne 1965: 372).

Radical skepticism can more convincingly escape the trap of self-contradictory assertion by eschewing assertive language altogether in adopting the language of fiction, which makes no knowledge-claims because it makes no assertions. Russell, the master logician, astutely deploys fiction to make manifest a truth that could not be directly asserted with consistency. Through fiction he can show what cannot logically be said. His radically skeptical views are made manifest by the action of the narratives themselves and are reinforced by the utterances of their fictional characters, which, again, are not real but only fictional assertions that communicate the alleged truths indirectly through the mouths of personae other than the author. Unlike Wittgenstein's philosophical theses of the *Tractatus* (Wittgenstein 1961: §6.54, 151), which lead to a higher understanding that shows them to be meaningless and worth throwing away, Russell's fiction need not be jettisoned as ultimately meaningless, even if nonassertive. If there are truths that one cannot assert with logical consistency, then literary fiction – through its status as nonassertive discourse – seems the best medium for communicating them. This idea gives an eminently logical content to the elusive and suspiciously mysterious notion of poetic truth that ordinary language cannot successfully assert but only literature can properly express.

Despite their striking differences of literary and lifestyles, of ethics and religious outlook, Russell shares with Eliot, Blanchot, and Bataille this notion of a special poetic or literary truth, otherwise inexpressible, that penetrates beyond logic to the depths of a dark, unfathomable reality.

Notes

1 On Eliot's philosophical training and views, see Richard Shusterman, *T.S. Eliot and the Philosophy of Criticism* (New York: Columbia University Press, 1988) and "Eliot as Philosopher," in A.D. Moody, *The Cambridge Companion to T.S. Eliot* (Cambridge: Cambridge University Press, 1994), 31–47.

2 For details on these Nobel prize awards, see https://www.nobelprize.org/prizes/literature/1948/eliot/facts/; https://www.nobelprize.org/prizes/literature/1950/russell/facts/.

3 Unlike Bataille, Blanchot, and Eliot, Russell did not write literary theory or aesthetics at all. Indeed, the questions of aesthetics find no place in his *History of Western*

Philosophy, and he repeatedly remarked that he had no understanding of aesthetics, confessing to his brother-in-law (the renowned art critic Bernard Berenson) that with respect to "the whole business about art ... I am a good British Philistine." E. Samuels, *Bernard Berenson* (Cambridge, MA: Harvard University Press, 1979), 385.

4 Bataille used the pseudonyms "Lord Auch" and "Pierre Angelique," respectively for *The Story of the Eye* and *My Mother*. For details on Bataille's life, which included some horrific childhood experiences, see his biography by Michel Surya, *Georges Bataille: An Intellectual Bibliography*, trans. K. Filjalkowski and M. Richardson (London: Verso, 2002).

5 My translation.

6 "It has been found again. / What? – Eternity. / It is the sea fled away / With the sun." From Oliver Bernard (trans.), *Arthur Rimbaud, Collected Poems* (London: Penguin, 1962), 217.

7 Bataille, however, was aware that poetry, like all art, can be appropriated to serve the utilitarian "project" of individuation and rationality through its emphasis on harmony. "In the fine arts, man makes 'real' the harmonious mode of existence inherent in project ... Harmony, like project, throws time back into the outside; its principle is the repetition through which all that is 'possible' is made eternal. The ideal is architecture, or sculpture, immobilizing harmony, guaranteeing the duration of motifs whose essence is the annulment of time" (Bataille 1954: 56).

8 For details on Blanchot's life see the extensive biography by Christophe Bident, *Maurice Blanchot: A Critical Biography*, trans. John McKeane (New York: Fordham University Press, 2018).

9 Blanchot's respect for the deep ontological meanings of death and absence resonates, of course, with Heidegger, who notes that "absence is not nothing; rather it is precisely the presence ... of the hidden fullness ... of Being." See Heidegger's letter of 18.6.1950 in Martin Heidegger, *Poetry, Language, Thought* (New York: Harper,1975), 182.

10 The dark, silent solitude of night that pervades Blanchot's fiction may reflect his habit of doing this writing always at night, as his days were mainly devoted to writing his critical essays through which he earned his living. Chronically ill from the age of 16, Blanchot also suffered from insomnia, "this way to 'make the night present'" (Bident 2018: 14).

11 For more on the ontological complexity of poetry, see Richard Shusterman, "Aesthetic Blindness to Textual Visuality," *Journal of Aesthetics and Art Criticism*, 41 (1982): 87–96.

12 For a detailed (but uncharitable) study of Russell's concern with isolation, madness, and death, see Roy Monk's two-volume biography, *Bertrand Russell: The Spirit of Solitude, 1872–1921* and *Bertrand Russell: The Ghost of Madness, 1921–1970* (New York: Free Press, 1996 and 2001). Monk also recounts how Russell's quest for love to relieve his anguish made him something of a sexual predator (taking Eliot's young wife as one of many prey).

13 Alan Wood, *Bertrand Russell: The Passionate Sceptic* (London: Routledge, 1957). For Russell's views on the knowledge/wisdom relationship, see Bertrand Russell, "Knowledge and Wisdom," in *Portraits from Memory, and Other Essays* (New York: Simon and Schuster, 1956).

14 It is important to note here that Eliot and Russell differed most strongly on the issue of religion, Russell insisting that "all the great religions of the world [are] both untrue and harmful," while Eliot saw religion as an indispensable element and source of culture. See Russell 2004: xxii and Eliot 1962: 13.

15 Russell knew he had a reputation "as a writer of doom" (Russell 1975: 527).

4 The Art of Writing in Chinese Thought

Self-Knowledge and Self-Cultivation in Early Chinese Philosophy

Our study of the role of literature and the act of writing in the practice of philosophy has ranged from ancient to twentieth-century thinkers, from Plato and Augustine through Montaigne, Wordsworth, and Kierkegaard to Bataille and Blanchot, Arendt and Beauvoir, T.S. Eliot and Bertrand Russell. We have focused on the Western tradition where philosophy emerged and developed from its Socratic definition as the loving pursuit of wisdom through efforts of self-knowledge and self-cultivation. But the West enjoys no monopoly on wisdom nor its pursuit through such efforts and the art of writing. Classical Chinese culture certainly shares these values and pursuits, though it lacks a figure identical to the Western concept of philosopher and who is similarly named. China's exemplary models of cultivation and wisdom are found in the ancient figures of the gentleman (君子 *junzi*), the scholar (士人*shiren*), the scholar-gentlemen-official (士大夫 *shidafu*) or more generally the literati (文人 *wenren* – literally persons of culture), and at the summit of wisdom, the sage (聖人 *shengren*).

Like the ancient Greek and Roman philosophers, traditional Chinese thinkers focused on the ethical problem of how to live, and they demonstrated the same striving for consummate wisdom and virtue through self-knowledge and self-cultivation. The *Analects* of Confucius (1:4) invokes the idea of examining thrice daily one's embodied self (三省吾身*san xing wu shen*), while the renowned third-century BCE Confucian Xunzi praises the cultivated gentleman for this inner focus: "Absorbed in the examination of his inner self, he will scorn mere external things" (Knoblock 1988: 154). Mencius, the second most important Confucian philosopher after the Master himself, likewise affirms the importance of cultivating his inner "flood-like qi" energy to develop mental and moral excellence (Lau 1970: 77). Another Confucian classic (thought to be authored by Confucius himself), *The Great Learning*, highlights self-cultivation (修身 *xiu shen*) as the key ethical foundation for harmoniously governing self, family, and society. "Their persons being cultivated, their families were regulated. Their families

DOI: 10.4324/9780429331770-4

being regulated, their states were rightly governed. Their states being rightly governed, the whole kingdom was made tranquil and happy" (Legge 1966: 313). The term *xiu shen* connotes also somatic cultivation because *shen*身 is the word for the human body as well as the human self or person. This essential embodiment of persons is implied (albeit more vaguely) in English because any somebody always involves (at least linguistically) "some body."

For Confucianism, music (which included poetry and dance) and ritual were crucial means of self-cultivation, partly because they centrally engaged and trained the body and thus educated also the emotions, which have an intrinsic somatic dimension. Confucius thus urged his disciples: "My young friends, why don't you study the [*Classic of Poetry* or *Book of*] *Songs*? Reciting the *Songs* can arouse your sensibilities, strengthen your powers of observation, enhance your ability to get on with others, and sharpen your critical skills" (*Analects* 17:9; Ames and Rosemont 1998: 206). Without studying ritual, one would not know "where to stand" or how to behave properly and with appropriate feelings in one's social interactions, as the broad goal of achieving harmony in both oneself and society "is the most valuable function of observing ritual" (1:12, 8:8: 74, 122).

The classical Daoist tradition similarly emphasizes self-cultivation with a somatic component. It interprets *xiu shen* (personal/bodily cultivation) less in terms of arts of refinement like music and poetry, but more in terms of *shou shen* (守身protecting the body) through arts of somatic health. These somatic arts include disciplines of breathing, diet, and exercise that formed the basis of traditional Chinese medicine. The great Daoist Zhuangzi (late fourth century BCE), noting that the ancient sages who "clarified the great Way" made sure to "cultivate their persons" (*xiushen*), urges us: "Diligently cultivate your [own] person [(*xiu shen*)] … [which means] not paying attention to externals" (Mair 1994: 123, 321). Zhuangzi combines both notions of cultivation in his advice: "Carefully guard your body [*shou shen*], and leave other things to prosper themselves. I guard the one so as to dwell in harmony. Thus have I cultivated my person [or body (*xiu shen*)] for one thousand two hundred years and my physical form has still not decayed" (Mair 1994: 96).

Chinese Culture and the Art of Writing

Unlike the dominant Platonic tradition of the West, classical Chinese thought did not see literature as a threat to wisdom and moral virtue; nor did it see the pursuit of these philosophical goals as somehow demanding a disregard for the body. Instead, somaesthetic engagement was key to the core philosophical quest for self-knowledge and self-cultivation that contributed to the broader goal of harmony that extended from the self to society to the natural world. With this differing emphasis on the somaesthetic dimension of self-cultivation comes a different approach toward the art of writing, a different form of engaging with that art and with the very act of writing itself. The distinctive approach to writing in Chinese theory derives not simply from its greater acceptance of embodiment, but from fundamental differences between the writing cultures of China and the West. The first difference is indeed the primacy of writing in the Chinese language. In contrast to Greek and the other Western languages of philosophy (as well as Sanskrit, the classical language of Indian philosophy), Chinese is not a phonetic language but one of ideographs. This means that unlike Greek and other Indo-European philosophical cultures, orality had no priority for thought. The written form, which was common throughout China, had primacy over oral expression. The latter could differ widely in different regions (and still does today in the oral differences between regional dialects, such as between Mandarin and Cantonese Chinese). As a consequence of its primacy, writing could not be seen as a dangerous supplement to the philosopher's thinking and speech; indeed, it was essential to such thought because it could communicate ideas more clearly, widely, faithfully, and transparently than speech could.

A second distinctive feature of traditional Chinese writing that has consequences for its expressive powers is that it uses a brush rather than a pen. Although the most ancient surviving examples of Chinese writings are engraved on surfaces (such as stone tablets or bones), by the time of the Han dynasty (206 BCE–220 CE) the brush became the common tool of writing on silk or paper. Its influence on Chinese culture grew to be enormous, inspiring the arts of poetry, calligraphy, and painting and more generally the literati culture that included philosophical reflection. The contrast between the Chinese culture of the brush and the Western culture of the stylus or pen is worth elaborating.[1]

Writing with a brush involves the same materials as the Chinese art of calligraphy: the brush applies black ink of varying density of color, produced by grinding an ink stick and mixing the grounds in water. Writing and calligraphy require similar skills and ordering in making brush strokes. Imprecision or improper order will result in ugly, illegible smears as the wet ink blurs and blotches. Brushes, traditionally made from bamboo for the stem and from some type of animal hair for the brush head, can provide different pictorial qualities because of their different sizes and materials; so do the different densities of ink and the different styles of brush strokes the artist applies. Even a single brush stroke of black ink can convey a variety of color shades and tonalities of expression. Thus, despite the simplicity of the media, the calligraphic brush and ink could produce an extraordinary range of expressive qualities and therefore became a leading option for the art of painting. Because its ink and water medium allows no erasing, crossing out, or going over, Chinese writing with the brush highlights spontaneity of expression, conveying directly the mood and energy of the writer's current thoughts and feelings through their traces in the gestural movement of his brush.

What the West calls calligraphy – whose etymology denotes "beautiful writing" as distinguished from normal writing – was in fact normal writing for traditional Chinese culture, though it was, of course, exceptional at its highest levels of skill. Calligraphic writing is designated by the Chinese term *shufa* (書法), which literally means "writing method."[2] But this does not imply that the visual beauty of such writing was not extremely important. Indeed, beauty and expressive quality in the brush strokes of one's writing were highly prized in the scholarly tradition of China. The fact that literary scholars had rigorous training and extensive practice in using brush and ink served to increase the prevalence of skills not only for calligraphy and painting but also for appreciating visual properties and meanings in the work of other artists. It enabled them to imbue their own literary writing with expressive painterly grace that communicated a personal flavor and energy, while enabling them to discern the qualities and changing mood and energy in the brushwork of others' writings. It moreover encouraged scholars to combine their brushed literary texts with brushed pictorial expression in a compound artwork of poetry, calligraphy, and painting. In the Confucian tradition of self-examination and self-cultivation through the arts, literary scholars could pursue knowledge, refinement, and harmonization of their persons through these three sister arts of the brush, which by the time of the Yuan dynasty (1368–1644) were firmly linked and known as "the three perfections" (*san jue* 三絕). The fundamental unity of calligraphy and painting was widely recognized and frequently asserted through the saying *shu hua tong yuan* (書畫同源), "calligraphy [or more broadly writing] and painting share the same origin" (Gao 1996: 82). Indeed, this common origin can be seen in the traditional Chinese characters for these terms *shu* 書 and *hua* 畫, whose top radicals are identical – suggesting a hand holding a brush – and whose bottom radicals are quite similar in form, with *shu*'s bottom connoting a writing surface like paper or silk, and *hua*'s connoting the division of a field.[3]

The masterful use of the brush in traditional Chinese writing is obviously an act of somatic skill different from the Western use of the pen. The brush is soft while the stylus or pen is hard and reflects its origin in inscribing marks by carving or penetrating a smooth wax surface. The word "stylus" – from which the Western concept of style derives – is based on the Latin word *stilus* meaning a pointed stake or hard-pointed instrument (often of metal) for writing on wax tablets. The French word for pen – *stylo* – obviously derives from this term, while the English word "pen" seems to derive from the Latin "penna" or "pinna" denoting a feather (whose hard-pointed tip serves the quill pen) or from a still older root of "pinna" in Proto-Indo-European language designating a sharp point. Etymologically, the Western concept of style developed from the stylus, a hard, inanimate writing tool, whereas the Chinese word for style is *fengge* 風格, whose root *feng* 風 means wind, suggesting moving spirit and life. The term *feng* also served to classify different types or styles of China's classic *Odes* according to the different ancient states from which they derived. More generally, *feng* as wind can be seen as the external expression of the *qi* (energy or breath) within a person. If the artist's inner *qi* creates the work as its external expression, this expression in turn exhibits that dynamic energy in terms of the work's *feng*, a style or atmosphere that conveys moving energy like the wind.[4]

In any case, the hard, narrow point of the stylus or pen can be contrasted to the softer brush. As Virginia Woolf laments, because "the pen is a rigid instrument ... it can say very little" (Woolf 2002: 37). In contrast, the brush can spread its ink more broadly, freely, and diversely. This enables not only more varieties of tone, line, and texture but also much more diverse and dynamic expressive qualities that such varieties of brushwork can convey. By using the center or tip of the brush, one makes a "'round' brushstroke" and achieves a thinner or finer line, whereas by using the edge of the brush, one gets a squarer effect (Fong 1992: 122). By holding the brush at middle point (*zhong feng*) or perpendicular to the paper, one gets a different effect than when one holds the brush in a slant (*pian feng*). When one presses the soft brush hard onto the paper, one gets a heavier effect than when one touches it only gently on the paper; and the same stroke may start out heavy and end lightly or vice versa, or be heavy in the middle and light at the ends or vice versa. Similarly, through the different ways the brush is dipped in ink, the single black ink can admit of different colors or shades that are traditionally described as "thick, thin, dry, and moist." In short, as Wen Fong argues, "Brush and ink, in their infinite line-and-surface, bone-and-flesh, hard-and-soft, and dry-and-wet combinations, can theoretically represent or signal everything in the universe," including, I would add, the many shades of meaning and feeling in the artist's heart and mind (122–3).

One way to appreciate the nuanced subtlety and variety of self-expression in the calligraphic and ink-wash painterly tradition is to compare it to a famous Western example of using the visuality of written inscription as a tool for self-examination and self-cultivation. Consider Benjamin Franklin's weekly table of 13 virtues "for Self Examination" (Figure 4.1), through which he would monitor himself with respect to these virtues by "marking every Evening the Faults of the Day" regarding each of them (Franklin 1986: 94, 98).[5]

Visually the diagram is very clear and plain – a clean, regular rectangular grid, whose intersecting straight black lines create blank white squares that provide space for the possible placing of discrete black circles or dots. There are no curving or diagonal lines, no wiggles, and no texturing. Moreover, the symbolic functioning of the ink marks here is very simple and abstract. The thickness of the lines, the size of the dots or circles, and their color or shade of black, all these carry no significance. The only functioning of the marks is simply being present in their place; abstractly identifying the days of the week, the 13 abstract virtues, and the existence of the day's occasions on which the person violated the virtue by committing a fault. There is nothing expressive of what it feels like to exhibit the virtue or to fail in it through faulty behavior. In stark contrast to the richly expressive visuality of calligraphy, Franklin's graphic tool of self-study and self-cultivation provides

FORM OF THE PAGES

Temperance.							
Eat not to Dullness *Drink not to Elevation.*							
	S	*M*	*T*	*W*	*T*	*F*	*S*
T							
S	●●	●		●		●	
O	●	●	●		●	●	●
R			●			●	
F		●			●		
I			●				
S							
J							
M							
Cl.							
T							
Ch.							
H							

Figure 4.1 Benjamin Franklin's Table of Virtues.

no nuanced sense of the author's personality, style, sentiments, energy, or current mood. Of course, the very design of the page shows Franklin's desire for order, clarity, and self-improvement, but there is no personal poetry or subtlety of self-expression. Rather than the human poignancy of expressive art, we get abstract, conceptual bookkeeping by the numbers. Franklin's method suggests a clear separation of morals from art and aesthetics, a division that grew sharper through nineteenth-century notions of art for art's sake. Such a division is antithetical to the Chinese tradition that made the aesthetic realms of art and ritual the very pillars of Confucian morality.

Chinese literati took the quality of their brushwork more seriously than Western writers valued their penmanship. If Western thinkers saw written words as merely material symbols for higher abstract thoughts, the Chinese valued them as fascinating traces of subtle, fleeting, personal qualities of feeling and mood that no abstract idea could capture. Although Montaigne took the utmost pains to examine himself in every possible way, reflecting as intensely as he could on his opinions and memories, he did not appreciate what he could learn of his former thoughts and moods from his past writings. He confessed his penmanship so poor as to claim: "I cannot even write so I can read it; so that I would rather do over what I have scribbled than give myself the trouble of unscrambling it" (Montaigne 1965: 487). Montaigne attributed his illegible writing to his general bodily clumsiness, but did not consider this failure in penmanship a blemish on his literary achievement. Chinese literati would not share such sentiments but would certainly converge with Montaigne in regarding the act of writing as a bodily affair.

The Somaesthetics of Chinese Writing

Mastery of the brush in Chinese writing involves distinctive somatic skill. The proper writing of a Chinese character is not simply a matter of producing the right visual appearance; proper form means the proper sequence of brush strokes made in the proper direction. Moreover, the creation of skilled brush strokes involves not only the hand wielding the brush but the soma (or *shen*身) as a whole: one's vision, one's posture and proprioceptive and kinaesthetic feelings, one's energy, balance, breathing, and emotions – all of which influence the quality of the brush stroke. The strongly somatic dimension of brush strokes helps explain why "people having no previous acquaintance with Chinese culture react to calligraphy with immediate, even visceral, excitement" (Hay 1983a: 74). They sense implicitly through their bodies the dynamic expression of the brush strokes despite not being able to read the characters. A Chinese scholar skilled in the art of the brush could read not only the characters he wrote but also the state of his own mind when he wrote them, merely by looking at the quality of his brush strokes. Similarly, by simply practicing his use of the brush (often by imitating exemplary models), he could increase his refinement.

Before exploring the role and powers of ink and brush for the philosophical ends of self-knowledge and self-cultivation, we should elaborate the somatic dimension of calligraphic brushwork. A key principle of this art is that brush strokes provide an external expression and artistic transformation of the creative energy or *qi* (氣) currently residing in the artist's body and guiding his use of the brush. Consider the bodily analogies of writing's key materials. If ink and water correspond to bodily fluids like blood and lymph, then the hair of the brush suggests human hair and skin, while the hard bamboo stem is likened to bone or more generally the skeletal frame. The union of brush and ink thus combines the body's hard and soft dimensions: its hard, skeletal frame together with its liquids and soft skin, hair, and flesh. Moreover, theorists describe the brush strokes themselves in somatic terms: not only as bones and flesh and blood, but also as arteries (*mai*), sinew (*jin*), and bone marrow (*sui*).[6] Though the brush hair is soft compared to the bamboo stem, the brush stroke itself is sometimes characterized as bone or sinew so as to contrast it to the ink which is likened to flesh. Here is a quote to that effect from the *Bizhentu* 筆陣圖, or *Battle Array of the Brush* by Wei Shuo, a famous female calligrapher who lived from 272 to 349:

> Calligraphy by those good in brush strength has much bone; that by those not good in brush strength has much flesh. Calligraphy that has much bone but slight flesh is called sinew-writing; that with much flesh but slight bone is called ink-pig. Calligraphy with much strength and rich in sinew is of sage-like quality; that with neither strength nor sinew is sick. Every writer proceeds in accordance with the manifestation of their digestion and respiration of energy.
>
> (Hay 1983a: 85)[7]

Beyond these matters of terminology, the energetic, dynamic somatic dimension of artistic brushwork is emphasized in the first two canons of Xie He's famous fifth-century treatise on the *Six Principles* of painting (六法 *Liufa*). The first canon or principle is "*qiyun shengdong*" (氣韻生動), which can be translated as rhythmic vitality or energy-resonating, life-giving movement; but *qi* (氣) also means breath, and *yun* (韻) means harmony as well as resonance. The second principle, "*gufa yongbi*" (骨法用筆) can be rendered quite literally as the bone method of using the brush, but it is more elegantly expressed as "skeletal patterning, using brush," where the brush stroke serves as the firm patterning instrument (around which the ink adheres as flesh) to express dynamic energy (Hay 1984: 103). The term *gu* (骨) is anatomically translated as "bone" but means something more and other than this in the dominantly physiological-functional (rather than anatomical) orientation of Chinese medicine. Not only does *gu* have a general structural role connected with skeletal bones, it also has the function of both storing and transmitting energy. That is why brushwork with superior energy is identified with bone.[8]

In the somaesthetics of Chinese writing, the requisite energy for good brushwork is not confined to the hand that holds the brush and the eyes and arms that guide its movements. Rather the whole body's energy is involved, so that the brushwork is indeed an expression of the body or person as a whole (recalling that the Chinese word *shen*身 means both body and person). Moreover, as a famous fable from Zhuangzi clearly suggests, the best brushwork derives from the energetic yet tranquil power that radiates from a confidently unstressed body.

> Lord Yuan of Sung wanted to have some pictures painted. The crowd of court clerks all gathered in his presence, received their drawing panels, and took their places in line, licking their brushes, mixing their inks, so many of them that there were more outside the room than inside it.

> There was one clerk who arrived late, sauntering in without the slightest haste. When he received his drawing panel, he did not look for a place in line, but went straight to his own quarters. The ruler sent someone to see what he was doing, and it was found that he had taken off his robes, stretched out his legs, and was sitting there naked. "Very good," said the ruler. "This is a true artist!"
>
> (Watson 1968: 228)

Here the artist's care for his body is presented as being even more essential for true artistry than is his care for his essential media of ink and brush and the drawing surfaces of silk and paper. The body, therefore, appears as the primary and essential medium for art as well as for life. Emphasizing the body's primordial importance by highlighting how the "true artist" strips down to nakedness, Zhuangzi shows that the whole body is important for painting by underlining the artist's action of leg-stretching rather than mentioning any preparatory exercise of the hand and eyes whose use is obviously crucial in the art of the brush. Besides evoking the idea of a relaxed posture, the pose of sitting naked with stretched-out legs suggests a body that can more directly absorb environing energy by being unclothed and having more contact with the ground, while also allowing the energy to circulate more freely by not having one's limbs bent or flexed.[9]

Self-Cultivation through the Art of Writing

From the Han dynasty to the end of the Qing in the twentieth century, China's arts of poetry, calligraphy, and philosophical reflection drew largely on the literati class. This was an intellectual elite also described as scholar-gentlemen or scholar-officials (士大夫 *shi dafu*), whose literary training and intense study of the Confucian classics were designed to get them high-ranking government jobs. However, many literati abandoned this career choice to focus on the arts, often because of distaste for the politics of the ruling government. Literati art flourished in the Yuan dynasty, after the Southern Song dynasty's final fall to the Mongolian conquest in 1279, because the policies of the new, Mongolian Yuan rule alienated much of the Confucian scholar-class from governmental service and thus spurred them to channel their energies and talents more narrowly into artistic pursuits, including that of painting.

In contrast to professional painters, supported by the Imperial court or wealthy patrons and focused on creating beautiful objects for sale, the literati painters were masters of writing and Confucian philosophy who primarily focused on the classical Confucian goal of self-cultivation.[10] The literati artists therefore painted more as a means of self-knowledge, self-expression, and self-refinement, much in the same way that they composed poetry or made music or wrote philosophical texts. It was all part of the Confucian melioristic quest for continuous cultivation. This difference of artistic approaches reflects the central distinction Aristotle made between *poiesis* and *praxis*, a distinction that greatly influenced the entire Western tradition of art by marginalizing art from the ethics of character and the practice of life. Art, claims Aristotle, is a form of making (*poiesis*) that has for its goal a finished object beyond the activity of making and outside the person who is the maker; its end and value being wholly in the object made. Action (*praxis*), on the other hand, has its end both in itself (the acts of action) and in the agent or actor, who is affected by how he acts, though allegedly not by what he makes.[11] If the goal of China's professional painters was to produce external objects for sale to others, the essential aim of the literati artists (whether in painting, calligraphy, or poetry) was to use the media and processes of artistic creation to express and refine their selves. Art and the ethics of self-cultivation were intimately, essentially connected.

This fundamental difference in purpose between professional artists and the literati was reflected in style. If commercial painters often sought to impress viewers through very large paintings with complex brush strokes and rich color, the literati style was much more modest and simple, specializing in plain ink and based on the brush strokes learned from calligraphy. Rather than striving to impress, the literati's goal in painting was to express with brushwork the artist's inner state and spirit or character. In the Yuan dynasty, this so-called "amateur" tradition became dominant in Chinese painting and was able "to hold that position for the remainder of the history of Chinese painting, except for a brief resurgence of the Academy tradition in the early Ming Period" (Cahill 1976: 4).

Having perfected their brushwork through the sister art of calligraphy, the literati painters often insisted on the fundamental unity of these two arts: not only by repeating the phrase *shu hua tong yuan*, but also by describing the act of painting in terms of the verb to write *xie* (寫) and sometimes by even praising good literati painting by calling it writing in contrast to the allegedly inferior academic painting style, which they called "depicting" (*miao* 描) and which they denigrated as being the style of "a vulgar craftsman" (Gao 1996: 168).[12] As the calligraphic tradition developed, the styles of some famous great calligraphers were preserved (sometimes even in stone carvings), and these stylistic models served as exemplars for aspiring literati to master. Such mastery involved self-cultivation through the absorption of the valued traditional styles, an absorption process that was distinctively somatic because it involved emulating the making of the brush strokes in their proper sequence of bodily movements (including the rhythmic and energetic dimensions of movement) rather than simply reproducing the character's visual shape or form. But such self-cultivation through emulation of masters also involved self-expression because the complex dynamics of the movement of brush and ink are always mediated by the particular somatic habits and current feelings of the artist. Brushwork therefore provided a means for the artist to express and read his own current mood or energetic state through its external pictorial manifestation in ink, a visual constellation whose meaning went far beyond the conceptual meaning of the words or objects painted by the brush. The goal was expressing subjective or spiritual truth not the objective representation or likeness of external things. Ni Zan writes, "I use bamboo painting only to write out the exceptional exhilaration in my breast, that is all. Why should I worry whether it shows likeness or not, whether the leaves are too dense or too sparse, or whether the branches are slanted or upright?" (Fong 1992: 487).

Although such graphological expressions of character, mood, and energy were principally done for the artist's own self-analysis and improvement, other expert artists and connoisseurs could analyze the brushstrokes to appraise the artist's character and feelings at the moment of creating the work, as well as his (or her) skill and style. Indeed, in the literati tradition, artistic quality was intimately connected to the artist's character and mind. As James Cahill explains:

> The literati artists believed ... that quality in a painting, the kind of painting that would be recognized by the sensitive connoisseur but might escape the ordinary viewer, derived from admirable qualities in the man who had created it and had little to do with techniques that could be learned.
>
> (Cahill 1976: 5)

Given this idea that "One 'saw the man in his painting,'" the literati artists sought to improve their personal, humanistic qualities through self-cultivation (Cahill 1976: 5). Therefore, the disciplines they pursued "were not those normally included in 'studying painting'" (5). Instead, "they comprised such matters as sharpening one's sense of style and becoming familiar with old styles through the study of antique paintings; perfecting one's brushwork, partly through the practice of the companion art of calligraphy; and refining one's perceptions and taste through constant, dedicated immersion both in nature and in the literati culture," which had the study of the Confucian philosophical classics as its core (5–6).

As poetry formed a crucial part of such culture and was closely linked with calligraphy and painting to constitute "the three perfections," the literati painters often "compos[ed] and inscrib[ed] poems to accompany ... their pictures" (18). Such poetic expression reinforced the basic tenet that literati artists regarded their works "as intimate statements of personal feeling" rather than merely pretty objects independent from one's personality (18). In pursuing their art as a form of self-expression aimed at self-knowledge and self-cultivation, they recognized that to best achieve these aims one should share these forms of self-expression with others who could provide constructive feedback on what they expressed. Painting, like writing, served as a personal "means of communication" (19). This is clear "not only from theoretical writings but also from many appreciatory inscriptions attached to paintings by ... later writers" and from the artists' own confessions (19).

The literati's expressive self-cultivation through artistic brushwork involved somaesthetic refinement because one's body – which Chinese medicine conceived not so much as an organization of physical things but as an organic field of energies – should be aesthetically reshaped through art's harmonies so that one's energies achieved better, more rewarding attunement. This could not only improve the artist's capacity to make finer artworks, but also render him a better human being. The practice of art, some theorists alleged, could not only make a person more attractive (radiating the harmonies established through his art), but also enable him to live better and even longer. Consider the following remarks by Wang Yu:

> By learning painting, people can cultivate a gentle disposition, cleanse the vexed temper, break the eccentric mood, release the restless drive, and admit the calm marrow. People in the past said that landscapists had long lives because they were fostered by vapor and cloud and there was nothing but vigor and vitality before their eyes. Since most of the great landscapists from ancient times down to today have enjoyed long lives, this might be true.
>
> (Gao 1996: 168)

Although these remarks sound extravagant, it remains a fact that each of the "so-called Four Great Masters of the late Yuan—Huang Kung-wang, Wu Chen, Ni Zan, and Wang Meng ... produced his finest work in his seventies or eighties," and that, more generally speaking, good artists, whether in painting or in calligraphy, were thought to improve with age (Fong 1992: 432).

If Chinese thinkers universally acknowledged that the arts of the brush were very useful for self-examination, self-knowledge, self-cultivation, and self-stylization, the reason could be that such arts enable the artist to situate her act of expression within larger contexts that are both personal and broadly cultural. To see how, we can focus solely on calligraphy as simply an act of writing (regardless of its specific conceptual content). By elaborating six ways in which the writer navigates between two contrasting aspects of calligraphy, we can see how she expresses her character or particular mood by how she negotiates these contrasts in her calligraphic performance.

First, there is the contrast between the established form of the Chinese character (which has a standardized number of strokes of a certain kind in a certain order) and, on the other hand, the specific writing style of the artist in using the brush. Second, there is the contrast between the popular or democratic nature of writing characters – all literate people can do it – and the superior, refined skill of expressive brush writing that the expert calligrapher develops through his training. Here the expert calligrapher embodies the ideal of a cultivated gentleman who both shares practices with common people but elevates those practices to a higher level of refinement, thus providing an exemplar for educating and leading the less refined without divorcing himself from them.

Third, as the making of conventionally defined characters involving an established procedural order, direction, and number of brush strokes that is learned through a process of repetitive training to improve efficiency in writing, calligraphy relies on the procedural muscle-memory of habit and thus, in one sense, is automatic. However, as an artistic expression, it involves the artist's spontaneity and free will; the repetitive habit is a background mechanism or skill on which the artist relies to expresses his spontaneous feelings and stylistic choices. In this way, one can say that calligraphic writing or *shufa* has *fa* (method) but is also something other than *fa*. Fourth, on the one hand, a calligrapher can have an enduring characteristic personal style or quality that is recognizable from one work to another (and even across the different generic calligraphic styles that he imitates). But, on the other hand, the writer's brushstrokes will express the varying contexts and changing energies or feelings that animate or inspire his particular use of the brush at the specific moment of writing. As visible indicators of the mood and energy that produce the brushstrokes, calligraphic writings provide the artist with a tool of self-knowledge, a measure of his somatic vitality, tranquility, and body-mind balance, just as it supplies a tool to cultivate or improve such balance by its channeling and regulating of energy and feeling.

A fifth contrast is premeditation versus spontaneity. Although the actual movement of the brush must be smoothly spontaneous rather than hesitating or halting with deliberation, its unforced flow of *qi* energy must be somewhat pre-structured by a specific artistic intention, meaning, or idea (which need not be a visual mental image or a propositional assertion) in the artist's mind. Hence, the Chinese saying "*yi zai bi xian* (意在筆先)" meaning "thought precedes brush." Wang Xizhi (303–61), who is often described as the sage of calligraphy, thus writes:

> Those who are going to do calligraphy usually concentrate and meditate quietly while pretending to grind the ink in order to develop in their minds the sizes, the postures, both horizontal and vertical, and the vibrations of the forms of the characters, and to make their sinew and vein (*jin mai* 筋脈) linked together. [First, to ensure that] *yi* precedes the brush, then to write the characters.
>
> (Gao 1996: 152)[13]

Zhuangzi's story of the artist preparing by sitting comfortably undressed on the floor with legs extended could suggest this calmly meditative preparation of realizing his *yi* (while nourishing his *qi*) before taking up the brush.

The sixth pair of calligraphic contrasts is tradition and innovation. The skilled artist deeply respects tradition and first develops his own talent by emulating the tradition's cherished exemplars, which guide him in the quest for self-cultivation. But as that quest entails the artist's own self-knowledge and refining self-stylization, calligraphic art likewise involves innovative self-expression that can create new styles. Ink-wash painting (which often contains calligraphic colophons or poems) displays the same blend of deeply respectful emulation of traditional styles, themes, and exemplars together with creative self-expression. In the same way, its use of the brush combines trained habit and spontaneity, enduring personal style and changing contexts of mood, energy, and qualities of ink, brush, and paper. Important contemporary Chinese artists such as Pan Gongkai integrate deep respect for tradition with stylistic (including technological) innovation.[14] However, we confine our study here to four seminal exemplars of literati from much earlier times who used their arts of the brush for philosophical self-examination and self-cultivation during the Yuan (1279–1368) and Ming (1368–1644) dynasties and to works that combine painting, poetry, calligraphic writing, and philosophical reflection. The four artists are Wu Zhen, Wang Meng, Ni Zan, and Shen Zhou.

Poetry, Painting, and Philosophical Reflection

Consider *The Poet on a Mountaintop* (Figure 4.2) by Shen Zhou (1427–1509), an influential artist of the Ming dynasty, thoroughly trained in the Confucian classics and deeply respectful of that tradition and its expression in the Yuan *shidafu* artistic styles.

Figure 4.2 Shen Zhou (1427–1509), *Poet on a Mountaintop.*

Along with its ink-wash landscape, the work includes a short poem whose English translation reads as follows:

> White clouds like a belt
> encircle the mountain's waist
> A stone ledge flying in space
> and the far thin road.
> I lean on my bramble staff
> and gazing into space
> Make the note of my flute
> an answer to the sounding torrent.
> (Sullivan 1974: 48)

Visually, the poet appears as a lone figure on an upwardly inclined mountain summit precipice, devoid of trees and overlooking a rocky cliff with clouds below and higher mountains in the distance, whose peaks emerge from the clouds that seem, like a white sash, to wrap the mountain's middle. Like the upward tilting ledge "flying" toward the space of distant mountains, the lonely literatus claims to gaze freely "into space." Ostensibly, according to the poem, his contemplative gaze is to the remote mountains and "the far, thin road" (perhaps suggesting the notion of life's long, narrow path). However, when we look at the painting, his gaze is focused directly on the calligraphic poem he has inscribed. In other words, the artist's contemplation of nature is in fact deeply reflective of himself; in looking at the landscape he examines himself through the self-expression of his painted poetry. This suggests that the contemplation of nature's beauties, if one's attention is thoughtful and heart-felt, will contain some reflection of who one is and one's relation to, or place in, the world. One can find oneself reflected in the mirror of nature because the Way (or *Dao*) runs through all things, and the artist's role in depicting nature should essentially include how nature affects his heart and mind, because that too belongs to nature's powers and beauties.

We should further remark that Shen Zhou's reflective contemplation here includes a distinct somaesthetic dimension. He notes his bodily condition of leaning on his bramble staff. If the position of leaning implies the bodily effort and fatigue of climbing to the mountain peak, then the dark bramble staff (since bramble connotes blackberry) evokes the tools that artistically support the calligraphic poet-painter-thinker by becoming the active extensions of his body – the staff-like writing/painting brush and black-colored ink of his art. To reinforce the core ideal of reflective self-cultivation through artistic self-expression, Shen Zhou's painting suggests that this project goes beyond the arts of the brush. The natural sound of the stream is answered and harmonized with the poet's playing of his flute, which is stick-shaped like a writing brush and which hangs on the belted waist of the poet's figure. Like the staff and the brush, the flute is gracefully incorporated as an extension of the artist's creative soma, endowed with his sensitivity and taste. We have here a philosophical vision of nature and art, of human life and inanimate things, unified in charming harmony.

The theme of contemplating nature as a means of artistic self-examination, self-expression, and harmonious self-cultivation was already prominent in the renowned Yuan dynasty literati artists. Consider *Red Cliffs and Green Valleys* (Figure 4.3) by Wang Meng (ca 1308–85).

Figure 4.3 Wang Meng (ca 1308–85), *Red Cliffs and Green Valleys.*

The painted image portrays the artist calmly seated on a riverbank and gazing over the tranquil water, attended by a boy who stands respectfully at some distance behind him, and surrounded by a few small objects evocative of the arts and of somaesthetic pleasures. The long tubular object on the artist's left side is probably meant to be a *qin* – a traditional lute-like musical instrument. That shape could also suggest a rolled up scroll of poetry or painting; the smaller round objects before him and to his right might be a teacup and teapot (with its stick-like handle) connoting gastronomic pleasures, but they may instead be a censer and a mini stove, suggesting the closely related beauties of smell. Whatever these objects are, they suggest aesthetic pursuits involving somatic skills and pleasures of the body that depend on the use of tools. The *qin*, like the brush, is a way of extending the soma and its aesthetic capacities through a tool that requires a well-trained body (whose cultivation involves more than skillful hands) to bring sonic harmonies that can complement the harmonies of smell and taste from the censer or tea set. Such instruments surrounding the contemplative scholar-artist suggest a philosophical idea central to Chinese culture: beauty and art belong not only to the distant, cerebral senses of sight and sound but serve and honor all the senses.

Water is nature's paradigm mirror, so Wang Meng's image of river contemplation immediately evokes self-reflection. The theme of self-examination is highlighted in the poem inscribed at the top right of the scroll, because it distinctly raises the existential questions of how he got to his present place, where he will go in the future, and if he will reach his goals in the brief time of human life.

> Far away, among a hundred thousand blue mountains,
> Vermilion cliffs and green valleys, deep and impenetrable.
> The wind through pine trees brings the sound of a waterfall from
> the edge of the sky;
> The scent of flowers emerges from the cave, pervading the clouds.
> When did the fishing boat bring me here?
> Where shall I meet the hermits of the Qin?
> Springtime is brief and flowers fall.
> Only the river flows, eastward, year after year.
>
> (Fong 1992: 461–2)

The poem celebrates the rich aesthetic experience of natural beauty that appeals to the body's diverse senses: lush colors for vision, fragrant scents that may be so pervasive one can almost taste them, the pleasing sounds of a waterfall brought by the wind, a wind that can be heard through the pines but also felt tactilely on one's skin.

As for the painted image, besides suggesting the sensory pleasures of art through the depicted implements, it deepens the themes of self-examination and self-cultivation through its placement of the boy's small, standing body behind the larger, seated artist-thinker. On the literal level, the boy seems a mere attendant follower, helping the man's efforts of cultivation. Metaphorically, however, he could represent the child that the artist once was but who now, having grown to adulthood, sits and examines himself – looking forward to where he will go and what he will become, but also looking backward to his youth, to who he has been and what he has done. If the artist's real eyes face forward to what he can still achieve, his mental eyes of contemplation also look back on what he has already accomplished by cultivating his talents, as the river of time inexorably passes. The poem's contemplative vision also expresses a wistfully utopian feeling, as its mention of the cave's pervasive scent of flowers, the fishing boat, and the hermits of the Qin unmistakably refer to the fisherman story of the famous Chinese "Peach Blossom" fable (*Taohua Yuan* 桃花源記) written by Tao Yuanming in 421. That utopian fable tells of a fisherman who accidentally sailed into a river whose banks were covered with peach petals and which ended in a cave whose passage led to a magically peaceful village. Established long before by people seeking reclusive refuge from the unhappy strife of the Qin dynasty, the village remained hidden and unknown, because its ensuing generations never wanted to renew contact with the troubled outside world.

The figure of the solitary fisherman roaming alone through natural landscapes became a familiar image for contemplative literati art, along with that of the meditative literatus himself and, in a sense, metaphorically representing him. Consider *Fisherman by a Wooded Bank* (Figure 4.4), a small but famous hand-scroll painting-with-poem by the renowned Yuan master Wu Zhen (1280–1354).

Figure 4.4 Wu Zhen (1280–1354), *Fisherman by a Wooded Bank.*

As Fong notes, the fisherman's figure, "briskly done in a few strokes and dots, is a marvel of abbreviation, while the rocks and trees, depicted with the same halting round blunt brushstrokes and clustered ink dots, bristle with energy and liveliness" (Fong 1992: 450). Above the fisher's forward-leaning figure, curved in concentrated thought, the artist brushes the following poem in a clear cursive script:

> Red leaves west of the village reflect evening rays,
> Yellow reeds on a sandy bank cast early moon shadows.
> Lightly stirring his oar,
> Thinking of returning home,
> He puts aside his fishing pole, and will catch no more.
> (450)

Caught between day and night, sun and moon, his work of fishing and the restful haven of home, the artist finds his mood of self-examining reflection magnified because the environing atmosphere of reflections comes not simply through the water but through the red leaves and yellow reeds that respectively reflect the setting sun's rays and the early moon shadows. The situation, moreover, is one of reflective deliberative decision: should he continue his day's labors or refresh himself by ending them? "Thinking of returning home," how does he perform this thinking? Not by empty-handed meditation, but by "lightly stirring his oar." Thinking is done through bodily action, and is proprioceptively felt through the body. This lightly stirring of the oar, moreover, makes a brilliant metaphor for self-expressive brushwork artistry in poetic writing and painting, which edifies while it entertains. The oar in water is like the brush in ink, or the inked brush on paper, skillfully guided by the person's hand and body but also guiding the person to a new position or condition of understanding.

Fong rightly claims, "As a symbol of reclusion, the leisurely fisherman was contrasted with the harassed official struggling to cope with the complexities of court life" (Fong 1992: 450). Moreover, in this particular work, we can also see the fishing pole (which, like the oar, is a stick skillfully moved in water) as symbolizing the brush and thus also the chores of the brush in official clerical work. Such work sharply contrasts with the free exercise of his brush in "lightly stirring" aesthetic pursuits of writerly or painterly self-cultivation and self-expression. We could then read the poem's idea of returning home in terms of the classical Chinese idea of self-cultivation as returning to oneself rather than seeking externals such as material wealth and worldly power. Indeed the poem, in the original Chinese, does not specifically mention the word "home"; its literal meaning is more general, something like "now to return perhaps."[15]

In the artworks thus far discussed, human bodies are pictorially represented. But traditional ink wash painting often conveys the themes of self-expression and self-cultivation without painting any human figures but instead symbolically suggesting them. The Yuan master painter-poet Ni Zan (1301–74) does this in two different ways. One method is by portraying empty dwellings that strongly evoke thoughts of human presence by highlighting its absence, as in Ni Zan's *Empty Pavilion in a Pine Grove* (Figure 4.5).

Figure 4.5 Ni Zan (1301–74), *Empty Pavilion.*

The painted pavilion is indeed empty, but the short poem he writes in on the upper left of the work pithily explains the deeply human reason for that absence while assuring the human's continuing presence.

> The pavilion stands under a tall pine tree;
> The recluse has departed after nightfall.
> When the morning comes, he shall return
> To dry his freshly washed hair in the rising sun.
> (Fong 1992: 485)[16]

The contemplative, enlightenment-seeking recluse must leave for the night to rest in the shelter of home so that he can return clean and refreshed to seek the light of truth in the morning with the rising sun. His freshly washed hair suggests the freshly rinsed hair of his writing brush as he prepares his quest for enlightening self-cultivation through expressive brushwork that the sunlight allows him to produce and scrutinize as a means of self-examination. The recluse absent from the pavilion could well be the artist himself, for we know Ni Zan enjoyed, and painted scenes from, "the scholar's pavilion retreat" (Fong 1992: 477). The devoted artist identifies with his instrument, the brush, as both "dry [their] freshly washed hair in the rising sun" (485). In the hermit's absence, the tall pine stands guard in his place, watching over "the pavilion [that] stands under" it (485). We further associate the pine tree with the reclusive seeker/artist, as both are the sort of living things that make the pavilion what it is. As human thought decides where to locate the pavilion while human energies and skills actually build it, so the substance of dead trees provides the wood for its construction, while the lovely living presence of overhanging trees (the painting shows a cluster of pines) helps determine the human decision to build it there. This composition of clustered trees, as Fong notes, repeats itself in many of Ni Zan's paintings and thus becomes "a symbol of himself and his world" (485).[17]

It reappears in his famous *Six Gentlemen* of 1345 (Figure 4.6), which exemplifies the second strategy of expressing human concerns without human images. This strategy functions by depicting natural objects whose figures stand for humans because they are somehow humanlike or have close human associations, such as sharing with humans the same context, conditions, or fate. The poem that Ni Zan's teacher (the renowned Huang Gongwang) brushed in at the top right of the painting explicitly links the six trees to literati gentlemen-scholars and gives the work its name:

> Distant cloudy mountains range across the autumn river;
> Nearby, ancient trees huddle by the sloping shore.
> Six gentlemen stand facing one another,
> Upright, straight, outstanding, unbending.
> (Hearn 2010: 236)

Figure 4.6 Ni Zan (1301–74), *Six Gentlemen*.

A sad, beleaguered cluster of six trees, having weathered the river's autumn flood, remain standing together face to face, isolated on a hill slope. This is a poignant symbol of the disenfranchised Confucian scholar class after the Mongol conquest, especially if we remember the Confucians' insistence on the "six arts" as the core of their educational philosophy.

I close this chapter by returning to the Ming master Shen Zhou whose *Night Vigil* of 1492 (Figure 4.7) demonstrates that the philosophical reflections of literati scholar-artists were not limited to brief bursts of poetic calligraphy on ink-wash painting evoking Confucianism's key themes of self-examination and self-cultivation.

Figure 4.7 Shen Zhou (1427–1509), Night Vigil.

Night Vigil's extended, tightly written prose discussion (around 550 words in English translation) takes almost as much space as its landscape (a small cluster of dwellings nestled beneath high mountains) painted below the text. Although its classical Confucian roots are evident, the essay has a distinctive hint of Daoist or Chan Buddhist Neo-Confucian thought in its celebration of spiritual enlightenment attained through quiet sitting meditation and its valorization of night's silence for cleansing the mind.

The text begins with a detailed account of the artist's experience after waking up from an enjoyably "sweet" sleep "on a cold night" and being "unable to go to sleep again" (Sullivan 1974: 52). After dressing and trying to read, he then tired and stopped reading and just "sat calmly doing nothing," absorbing the night's surrounding "silence" and the "fresh brightness" of "a pale moon" that had followed a "long rain" (52). "Then after a long time" of absorbing the silence and cleansing his mind with refreshing emptiness, he "gradually became aware of sounds" that distracted him with various feelings (52). "The rustling of the wind stirring the bamboo gave one the feeling of going bravely and unwavering onward"; the "snarling of dogs gave feelings of barring out evil, of opposing marauders"; "the sound of drums ... stirred restless thoughts that were lonely and sad," including "the official drum" marking time and beating "gradually faster, hastening the dawn," until "the sound of a bell [raised] ... thoughts of waiting for the dawn, rising and doing [the duties of the day]. It was inevitable" that the night's calm meditative state was eventually broken as daytime thoughts encroached, so Shen Zhou turns from mind-cleansing meditation to philosophical reflection through writing, by recording his experience and analysis of his nocturnal meditation (52).

He avows his inclination and habit "to enjoy sitting in the night," often starting by reading a book but "usually stopping at the second watch" (approximately 10pm to midnight), because in reading "the mind is bent on learning" so it cannot be properly purified (52). Moreover, the outside "clamour is not at rest" until after midnight. Mind purifying meditation requires both "the outside calm and the inner world at peace," and Shen Zhou found them both that particular night, when "all sounds and shapes [were initially able to] bring this stability and calm," and "thus can one purify the mind and spirit and realize one's will" (*zhiyi*) (52).

Shen Zhou then extends his philosophical reflection further into central topics of epistemology and ontology. He argues that how we perceive and respond to sounds, shapes, and other appearances of things depends on the state of our minds and the degree of our mind's subjugation to such appearances. He claims "that appearance is the servant of a thing [outside the mind], and yet the mind hastens to follow it," so the mind is led astray to be enslaved by illusion and external things, but when properly cleansed can sense without such enslavement (52). From this point in the essay, Shen

Zhou's philosophical reflection becomes so dense with richly suggestive ideas that I should cite it in full:

> True perception through hearing lies concealed in sound like that of drum and bell, whereas perception through seeing is hidden in any pattern. Thus things usually harm rather than help men. Often is it like tonight's sounds and shapes, for they are really no different from other times, and yet striking the ear and eye they become so firmly and wonderfully a part of me. And so this existence of sounds and patterns is not what prevents me from gaining wisdom; for things are not enough to enslave men.
>
> When sound is broken and shape shattered and the will rises free, what is this will? Is it within? Or is it without? Or is it in a thing? Or does it cause the thing to be? Is there not a way of defining the difference? Most certainly, and I perceive the difference.
> How great is the strength to be gained sitting in the night. Thus, cleansing the mind, waiting alone through the long watches by the light of a candle becomes the basis of an inner peace and of an understanding of things. This, surely, will I attain.
>
> (55)

Shen Zhou does not here elaborate his answers to these questions or elucidate "the difference" he perceives (55). Perhaps he felt his deeper "understanding of things" was conceptually ineffable, yet somehow expressed through the calm, stable characters of his calligraphy and the tranquil landscape painted beneath with the solitary, serenely seated human figure at its dramatic center (55).[18] Perhaps, through his nocturnal meditation, Shen Zhou grasped Laozi's silent Daoist truth and thus refused to formulate wisdom that cannot properly be said or written. "One who knows does not speak; one who speaks does not know" (*Daodejing* LVI.128; Lau 1963: 63).

Following that interpretive direction, we might conclude our study with the familiar, if paradoxical, warning: *Caveat lector*. The language of literature and philosophy can deceive as well as instruct, especially in writing, as Plato long ago insisted (recall his arguments from Chapter 1). More generally, it is easier to lie in writing than in face-to-face direct speech; it is even more difficult to lie in body language. By being a more somatically sensitive form of writing than typing or using a pen, calligraphic composition with a brush may more honestly express the writer's feelings, even those feelings of which the writer is not aware. Calligraphy can surely express qualities of feeling and meaning that printed texts cannot capture or communicate.

Technologies for composing texts (oral utterance, pen, pencil, brush, typewriter, or computer) are not merely external instrumentalities for recording thoughts but tend to shape the thoughts they present. If Plato contrasted orality with writing, later thinkers contrasted writing by hand with typing.

When Nietzsche's failing eyesight compelled him to compose with a typewriter, he noticed how it modified his style and thought. "Our writing tools are also working on our thoughts," he told a friend (Kittler 1999: 200).[19] T.S. Eliot made a similar observation, that the typewriter compressed his thinking into a tighter style.

> Composing on the typewriter, I find that I am sloughing off all my long sentences which I used to dote upon. Short, staccato, like modern French prose. The typewriter makes for lucidity, but I am not sure that it encourages subtlety.
>
> (Eliot 1988: 144)

Today computers reshape thought and writing far more aggressively, as programs like Google's Smart Compose instruct you how to complete your thought by predicting what you intend to say, while the program Grammarly tells you that your sentence is too long or needs rephrasing. As writing is a key technology for self-knowledge and self-cultivation, so new technologies of writing (by shaping our thinking and feeling) may reshape philosophy's art of living.

If writing with the calligraphically skilled body increasingly disappears in Asian cultures, while penned letters and poetry similarly die out in the West, then certain qualities of subtle feeling and nuanced meaning will vanish from literary and philosophical culture. Will visual culture fill this gap? If so, it will need more than the digital emoji. We may need a reinvestment in the expressive somaesthetic power of the human voice and somatic gesture and performance to enrich the practice of literature and philosophy.[20] Philosophy's art of living may always require the art of writing, but it also needs more than words to realize its full and most rewarding potential for human flourishing.

Notes

1 It is worth mentioning here the existence of more recent writing tools like typewriters and computer keyboards that contemporary authors have often used. However, of the four contemporary twentieth-century authors discussed in Chapter 4, only Eliot seems to have composed with a typewriter. Russell apparently never himself used a typewriter for composing, but he sometimes dictated texts to typists. There is no evidence that Blanchot and Bataille ever composed with a typewriter. I base these remarks on email messages from two Eliot scholars (Lyndall Gordon and Ronald Schuchard), from the Russell expert Nicholas Griffin, and from the biographies of Bataille and Blanchot cited in Chapter 4.

2 Chinese has another word for "writing" (*xie* 寫) that is more commonly used.

3 For more details on some of these points, see James Cahill, *Hills beyond a River: Chinese Painting of the Yuan Dynasty, 1279–1368* (New York: John Weatherhill, 1976); Wen C. Fong, *Beyond Representation: Chinese Painting and Calligraphy, 8th–14th Century* (New Haven: Yale University Press, 1992); Michael Sullivan, *The Three Perfections: Chinese Painting and Calligraphy* (London: Thames and

Hudson, 1974); and Jianping Gao, *The Expressive Act in Chinese Art: From Calligraphy to Painting* (Uppsala: Uppsala University Press, 1996).

4 Individual personal writing styles in calligraphy sometimes became so influential that their names were extended to define a more general style, for example Zhao-ti, Ou-ti, Yuan-ti. In being designated with the term "*ti*" (體), which is a word signifying body and used to refer to the human body's four limbs (*si ti*), these style names suggest the intimate link of calligraphy to the body.

5 The virtues are Temperance, Silence, Order, Resolution, Frugality, Industry, Sincerity, Justice, Moderation, Cleanliness, Tranquility, Chastity, and Humility. Benjamin Franklin, *The Autobiography and Other Writings* (London: Penguin, 1986), 91–2.

6 Hay provides a detailed account of this in terms of traditional Chinese medicine in "The Human Body and Calligraphy," in Susan Bush and Christian Murck (eds.), *Theories of the Arts in China* (Princeton, NJ: Princeton University Press, 1983a), 74–102.

7 Compare the remark of Zhang Huaiguan (713–41) "A horse is considered superior when it has much sinew and little flesh, inferior when it has much flesh and little sinew. Calligraphy is also like this" (Hay 1983a: 91). Note also the remark of a Yuan dynasty writer, Chen Yiceng, who claims "Characters are born from ink, ink is born from water; water is the blood of characters" (Hay 1983a: 96).

8 I draw here on the detailed analysis of these two principles and their relation to Chinese medicine from John Hay, "Values and History in Chinese Painting, I," *Res: Anthropology and Aesthetics*, 6 (1983b), 72–111; and John Hay, "Values and History in Chinese Painting, II," *Res: Anthropology and Aesthetics*, 7/8 (1984), 102–36.

9 This striking anecdote acquired great prominence in the ink-wash tradition because it highlighted the genre's distinctive somatic dimension. Its verbal image of disrobing and stretching oneself out naked *jieyi panbo luo* (解衣盘礴裸) shortened to *jieyi panbo* was transformed into a term frequently used in painting and calligraphic criticism to describe the bodily performative process of artistry, including its initial stages before the artist applies his brush to ink and paper. Certain popular painters attracted crowds wishing to witness the somatic dimension of their painterly performance rather than just imagining it from its traces in the completed work. For many painters in this genre, a key element of preparation was absorbing the spirit of the objects to be painted, which sometimes involved somatically identifying with those objects through posture or gesture. See Gao 1996: 82–3.

10 This does not mean that literati never profited from the sale of calligraphy. The famous scholar and calligrapher Fu Shan (1607–84) was swamped with commissions for his calligraphy and apparently sometimes employed a ghost calligrapher to help him. See Bai, Qianshen, *Fu Shan's World: The Transformation of Chinese Calligraphy in the Seventeenth Century* (Cambridge, MA: Harvard University Press, 2003).

11 See Aristotle, *Nicomachean Ethics*, Book VI, 1140a1–1140b25, in Richard McKeon (ed.), *The Basic Works of Aristotle* (New York: Random House, 1968), 1025–7.

12 The ninth-century Chinese scholar, calligrapher, and painter Zhang Yanyuan wrote in his book of art history (*Lidai Minghua* Ji, 歷代名畫記 *Famous Paintings of the Past*) "Writing and painting have different names but a common body" (Sullivan 1974: 11). The Yuan master Ni Zan claimed: "Calligraphy and painting work the same way … It is said that a stroke of painting is just like a stroke of calligraphy. Each brushstroke must look backward and forward in a spirited manner, the stroke continuous without breaking off" (Fong 1992: 487).

13 The Wang Xizhi quote is from Gao 1996: 152, but with a slight grammatical adjustment of its last sentence.

14 For analysis of Pan Gongkai's work, see Richard Shusterman, "Somaesthetics and Self-Cultivation in Chinese Art," in E. Fischer-Lichte and B. Wihstutz (ed.), *Transformative Aesthetics* (London: Routledge, 2017b), 83–109.

15 The Chinese reads: 红叶村西夕照余，黄芦滩畔月痕初。轻拨棹，且归欤，挂起渔竿不钓鱼.

16 Fong notes Ni Zan's insistence on good poetry's need to be pithy and practical. It "never wastes a single sentence without saying something meaningful, never devotes [itself] to decoration alone" and "is like silk, hemp, and grain, which are useful in the world" (Fong 1992: 486).

17 The symbolic identification of the tree with the artist is further suggested in a colophon poem that a colleague inscribed on the upper right side of the work. It says of the recluse/artist: "Above all, he loves the tall pine tree" (translated in Fong 1992: 485).

18 The title of the essay in Chinese is simply "Record of a Night Sitting" 夜坐圖. I cite from the translation in Sullivan 1974: 52, 55.

19 The original German is: "unser Schreibzeug arbeitet mit an unseren Gedanken" and appears in Nietzsche's collected letters in *Nietzsche, Briefwechsel: Kritische Gesamtausgabe*, Giorgio Colli and Mazzino Montinari (ed.), (Berlin: de Gruyter, 1981), vol.1, 172 or at http://www.nietzschesource.org/#eKGWB/BVN-1882,202.

20 I explore the idea of a silent philosopher who expresses thought through gesture in my work with the Man in Gold, a project of performance art that extends into literature and philosophy. One of its products is the illustrated novella, *The Adventures of the Man in Gold* (Paris: Hermann, 2016) that also aims to revive the genre of the philosophical tale, which was an appealing, influential form of philosophical writing in the eighteenth century. For analysis of the Man in Gold's philosophical meanings, see my papers "The Philosopher without Words: Philosophy as Performative Art with *L'homme en Or*," in Curtis L. Carter (ed.), *Unsettled Boundaries: Philosophy, Art, Ethics East/West* (Milwaukee: Marquette University Press, 2017a), 36–50; and "Aesthetic Experience at the Borders of Art and Life: The Case of the Man in Gold," *Eidos: A Journal for Philosophy of Culture*, 5:2 (2021), 103–111. See also the six chapters on the Man in Gold in Jerold Abrams (ed.), *Shusterman's Somaesthetics: From Hip Hop Philosophy to Politics and Performance Art* (Leiden: Brill, 2022); and the reviews of *The Adventures of the Man in Gold* collected at http://www.fau.edu/artsandletters/humanitieschair/books/man-in-gold/man-in-gold-reviews/.

Works Cited

Abrams, Jerold (ed.) (2022), *Shusterman's Somaesthetics: From Hip Hop Philosophy to Politics and Performance Art*, Leiden Brill.

Abrams, M.H. (1986), "The Fiction of the Self," in H. Bloom (ed.), *William Wordsworth's The Prelude*, New York: Chelsea House.

Ames, Roger and Henry Rosemont (trans.) (1998), *The Analects of Confucius: A Philosophical Translation*, New York: Ballantine.

Arendt, Hannah (1997), *Rahel Varnhagen: The Life of a Jewess*, Baltimore, MD: Johns Hopkins University Press.

Aristotle (1968), *The Basic Works of Aristotle*, Richard McKeon (ed.), New York: Random House.

Augustine (1888), "The Soliloquies of St. Augustine," in Philip Schaff (trans.), *A Select Library of the Nicene and Post-Nicene Fathers of the Christian Church: First Series*, Buffalo: Christian Literature Co.

——— (1947), *On Music: De Musica*, in Robert Catesby Taliaferro (trans.), *The Fathers of the Church, Volume 4*, Washington, DC: Catholic University of America Press.

——— (1948a), *Answer to Skeptics: Contra Academicos*, in Denis J. Kavanagh (trans.), *The Fathers of the Church, Volume 5*, Washington, DC: Catholic University of America Press.

——— (1948b), *Divine Providence and the Problem of Evil: De Ordine*, in Robert P. Russell (trans.), *The Fathers of the Church, Volume 5*, Washington, DC: Catholic University of America Press.

——— (1993), *Confessions*, F.J. Sheed (trans.), Indianapolis, IN: Hackett.

Bacon, Francis (1845), "Of Truth," in B. Montagu (ed.), *The Essays or Counsels, Civil and Moral, and Wisdom of the Ancients*, London: William Pickering.

Bai, Qianshen (2003), *Fu Shan's World: The Transformation of Chinese Calligraphy in the Seventeenth Century*, Cambridge, MA: Harvard University Press.

Bataille, Georges (1947), "Joseph Conrad," *Critique*, 18, pp. 463–467.

——— (1954), *Inner Experience*, L.A. Bodlt (trans.), Albany, NY: SUNY Press.

——— (1985), "Emily Bronte," in A. Hamilton (trans.), *Literature and Evil*, New York: Marion Boyars.

——— (1987), *Story of the Eye*, Joachim Neugroschel (trans.), San Francisco, CA: City Lights Books.

——— (1995), *My Mother, Madame Edwarda, The Dead Man*, A. Wainhouse (trans.), London: Marion Boyars.

——— (2012), *Eroticism*, London: Penguin.

Beardsley, Monroe (1970), *The Possibility of Criticism*, Detroit: Wayne State University Press.

Beauvoir, Simone de (1959), *Memoirs of a Dutiful Daughter*, New York: Harper.

——— (1989), *The Second Sex*, New York: Vintage.

Bennet, Andrew (2003), "Wordsworth Writing," *The Wordsworth Circle*, 34(1), pp. 3–8.

Bident, Christophe (2018), *Maurice Blanchot: A Critical Biography*, John Mckeane (trans.), New York: Fordham University Press.

Bigelow, Patrick (1987), *Kierkegaard and the Problem of Writing*, Tallahassee, FL: University of Florida Press.

Blanchot, Maurice [1941] (1978), *Death Sentence*, L. Davis (trans.), Barrytown, NY: Station Hill Press.

——— [1941] (1988), *Thomas, the Obscure*, R. Lamberton (trans.), Barrytown, NY: Station Hill Press.

——— (1989), *The Space of Literature*, A. Smock (trans.), Lincoln: University of Nebraska Press.

——— (1995), *The Work of Fire*, C. Mandell (trans.), Stanford, CA: Stanford University Press.

——— (2001), *Faux Pas*, C. Mandell (trans.), Stanford, CA: Stanford University Press.

Brennan, Brian (1988), "Augustine's *De Musica*," *Vigiliae Christianae*, 42, pp. 267–281.

Brown, Peter (2000), *Augustine of Hippo: A Biography*, Los Angeles, CA: University of California Press.

Cahill, James (1976), *Hills Beyond a River: Chinese Painting of the Yuan Dynasty, 1279–1368*, New York: John Weatherhill.

Cavell, Stanley (1994), *A Pitch of Philosophy: Autobiographical Exercises*, Cambridge, MA: Harvard University Press.

Coleridge, S.T. (2002), *Collected Letters*, E.L. Griggs (ed.), Oxford: Oxford University Press, 2.

Danto, Arthur (1984), "Philosophy as/and/of Literature," *Grand Street* 3, p. 3.

Diogenes Laertius (1972), *Lives of Eminent Philosophers*, R.D. Hicks (ed.), Cambridge, MA: Harvard University Press.

Dover, K. J. (1978), *Greek Homosexuality*, Cambridge, MA: Harvard University Press, pp. 94–103.

Eliot, T.S. (1957), *On Poetry and Poets*, London: Faber.

——— (1962), *Notes Towards the Definition of Culture*, London: Faber.

——— (1964a), *Knowledge and Experience in the Philosophy of* F.H. Bradley, London: Faber.

——— (1964b), *The Use of Poetry and the Use of Criticism*, London: Faber.

——— (1969), *The Complete Poems and Plays of T.S. Eliot*, London: Faber.

——— (1976a), *For Lancelot Andrewes*, London: Faber.

——— (1976b), *The Sacred Wood*, London: Methuen.

——— (1976c), *T.S. Eliot Selected Essays*, London: Faber.

——— (1978), *To Criticize the Critic*, London: Faber.

——— (1988), *The Letters of T. S. Eliot*, vol. 1, 1898–1922, Valerie Eliot (ed.), New York: Harcourt Brace Jovanovich.

Engelmann, Paul (1967), *Letters from Ludwig Wittgenstein, with a Memoir by Paul Engelmann*, B. F. McGuinness (ed.), Oxford: Blackwell.

Epictetus (1992), *The Handbook*, Nicholas White (trans.), Indianapolis, IN: Hackett.

Foley, Michael (2015), "The Quarrel Between Poetry and Philosophy in the Early Dialogues of St. Augustine," *Philosophy and Literature*, 39, pp. 15–31.

Fong, Wen C. (1992), *Beyond Representation: Chinese Painting and Calligraphy, 8th–14th Century*, New Haven, CT: Yale University Press.

Foucault, Michel (1972), *The Archeology of Knowledge*, New York: Pantheon.

——— (1988), *Technologies of the Self: A Seminar with Michel Foucault*, Huck Gutman, Patrick H. Hutton, and Luther H. Martin (eds.), Amherst: University of Massachusetts Press.

——— (2011) "The Courage of the Truth (The Government of Self and Others II)," in G. Burchell (trans.), *Lectures at the Collège de France*, London: Palgrave Macmillan.

Frame, Donald (1965), "Introduction," in *The Complete Essays of Monaigne*, Stanford: Stanford University Press.

Franklin, Benjamin (1986), *The Autobiography and Other Writings*, London: Penguin.

Gao, Jianping (1996), *The Expressive Act in Chinese Art: From Calligraphy to Painting*, Uppsala: Uppsala University Press.

Garff, Joachim (2005), *Søren Kierkegaard: A Biography*, Princeton, NJ: Princeton University Press.

Gill, Stephen (1989), *William Wordsworth: A Life*, Oxford: Oxford University Press.

——— (ed.) (2008), *William Wordsworth The Major Works*, New York: Oxford University Press.

Goethe, J.W. von (1955), *Zur Naturwissenschaft im Allgemeinem in Goethes Werke*, 13, Hamburg: Christian Wegner Verlag.

——— (1966), *Maximen und Reflexionen*, in Goethes Werke (ed.), 12, Hamburg: Christian Wegner Verlag.

Grosart, Alexander B. (ed.) (1876), *The Prose Works of William Wordsworth, vol 2*, London: Edward Moxon, Son, and Co. 1 Amen Corner, Paternoster Row.

Habermas, Jurgen (1970), "Towards a Theory of Communicative Competence," *Inquiry* 13, pp. 360–375.

——— (1975), *Legitimation Crisis*, Thomas McCarthy (trans.), Boston, MA: Beacon Press.

Hadot, Pierre (1995), *Philosophy as a Way of Life*, Michael Chase (trans.), Malden, MA: Blackwell.

Hannay, Alistair (2001), *Kierkegaard: A Biography*, Cambridge: Cambridge University Press.

Hay, John (1983a), "The Human Body and Calligraphy," in Susan Bush and Christian Murck (eds.), *Theories of the Arts in China*, Princeton, NJ: Princeton University Press, pp. 74–102.

——— (1983b), "Values and history in Chinese Painting, I," *Res: Anthropology and Aesthetics* 6, pp. 72–111.

——— (1984), "Values and history in Chinese Painting, II," *Res: Anthropology and Aesthetics* 7/8, pp. 102–36.

Hearn, Maxwell (2010), "Poetry and Calligraphy Under the Mongols," in J.C.Y. Watt (eds.), *The World of Khubilai Khan: Chinese Art in the Yuan Dynasty*, New York: Metropolitan Museum of Art, pp. 181–240.

Hegel, G. W. F. (1991), *Elements of the Philosophy of Right*, Allen Wood and H.B. Nisbit (eds.), Cambridge: Cambridge University Press.

Heidegger, Martin (1975), *Poetry, Language, Thought*, A. Hofstadter (trans.), New York: Harper.

James, William (1907), *Pragmatism: A New Name for Some Old Ways of Thinking*, New York: Longmans.

——— (1999), "Letter to Miss Grace Norton," in I.K Skrupskelis and E.M. Berkeley (eds.), *The Correspondence of William James*, 7, Charlottesville, VA: The University Press of Virginia.

Kant, Immanuel (1996), *The Metaphysics of Morals*, Mary Gregor (trans.), Cambridge: Cambridge University Press.

Kierkegaard, Søren (1909–1920), *Papirer*, P.A. Heiberg and V. Kuhr (eds.), Copenhagen: Gyldendalske.

——— (1936), *Philosophical Fragments*, David Swenson (trans.), Princeton, NJ: Princeton University Press.

——— (1941), "The Sickness unto Death," in Walter Lowrie (trans.), *Fear and Trembling and The Sickness unto Death*, Princeton, NJ: Princeton University Press.

——— (1962), *The Point of View for My Work as an Author: A Report to History and related Writings*, Walter Lowrie (trans.), New York: Harper.

——— (1987), *Either/Or*, Part 1, Howard V. Hong and Edna H. Hong (trans.), Princeton, NJ: Princeton University Press.

——— (1993), *The Diary of Søren Kierkegaard*, Peter Rohde (ed.), New York: Citadel Books.

——— (2003), *Fear and Trembling*, Alastair Hannay (trans.), New York: Penguin Group.

——— (2010), *Concluding Unscientific Postscript*, Alistair Hannay (trans.), Cambridge; Cambridge University Press.

Kittler, Friedrich (1999), *Gramophone, Film, Typewriter*, G. Winthrop-Young and M. Wutz (trans.), Stanford, CA: Stanford University Press.

Knoblock, John (trans.) (1988), "On Self-Cultivation," in *Xunzi: A Translation and Study of the Complete Works*, 1, Stanford, CA: Stanford University Press.

Lau, D. C. (trans.) (1963), *Dao de Jing*, London: Penguin.

——— (trans.) (1970), *Mencius*, London: Penguin.

Legge, James (trans.) (1966), *The Four Books: Confucian Analects, The Great Learning, The Doctrine of the Mean*, and *The Works of Mencius*, New York: Paragon Book Reprint.

Mair, Victor (1994), *Wandering on the Way: Early Taoist Tales and Parables of Chuang Tzu*, Honolulu, HI: University of Hawai'i Press.

Marcus Aurelius (1964), *Meditations*, Maxwell Staniforth (trans.), London: Penguin.

Monk, Roy (1996), *Bertrand Russell: The Spirit of Solitude, 1872–1921*, New York: Free Press.

——— (2001), *Bertrand Russell: The Ghost of Madness, 1921–1970*, New York: Free Press.

Montaigne, Michel (1965), *The Complete Essays of Montaigne*, Donald Frame (trans.), Stanford, CA: Stanford University Press.

Nietzsche, Friedrich (1954), "On Truth and Lie in an Extra Moral Sense," in Walter Kaufmann (ed.), *The Portable Nietzsche*, New York: Vintage.

——— [1873] (1976), *The Portable Nietzsche*, Walter Kauffman (ed.), New York: Penguin.
——— (1981), *Nietzsche Briefwechsel: Kritische Gesamtausgabe*, G. Colli and M. Montinari (ed.), Berlin: de Gruyter.
——— (1992), *Nietzsche Ecce Homo*, R.J. Hollingdale (trans.), London: Penguin.
——— (1994),"Schopenhauer as Educator," in R.J. Hollingdale (trans.), *Untimely Meditations*, Cambridge: Cambridge University Press.
——— (1999a), *"Schopenhauer als Erzieher," "Ueber Wahrheit und Luege im aussermoralischen Sinne," and Ecce Homo*, G. Colli and M. Montinari (eds.), Berlin: de Gruyter.
——— (1999b), *The Birth of Tragedy*, R. Geuss and R. Speirs (eds.), Cambridge: Cambridge University Press.
NobelPrize.org (2021), "Bertrand Russell – Facts," Nobel Media AB 2021. Wed. 17 Mar 2021. https://www.nobelprize.org/prizes/literature/1950/russell/facts/
NobelPrize.org (2021), "T.S. Eliot – Facts," Nobel Media AB 2021. Mon. 15 Mar 2021. https://www.nobelprize.org/prizes/literature/1948/eliot/facts/
Nussbaum, Martha (1994), *The Therapy of Desire*, Princeton, NJ: Princeton University Press.
Plato (1925), *Ion*, in trans. H.N. Fowler, W.R.M. Lamb, R.G. Bury, and Paul Shorey (eds.), *Plato in Twelve Volumes*, Cambridge, MA: Harvard University Press.
——— (1925), *Phaedrus*, in trans. H.N. Fowler, W.R.M. Lamb, R.G. Bury, and Paul Shorey (eds.), *Plato in Twelve Volumes*, Cambridge, MA: Harvard University Press.
——— (1966), *Apology*, in Harold North Fowler (trans.), *Plato in Twelve Volumes*, Vol. 1, Cambridge, MA: Harvard University Press.
——— (1966), *Crito*, in Harold North Fowler (trans.), *Plato in Twelve Volumes*, Vol. 1, Cambridge, MA: Harvard University Press.
——— (1969), *Republic*, in Paul Shorey (trans.), *Plato in Twelve Volumes*, Cambridge, MA: Harvard University Press.
——— (1997), *Plato: Complete Works*, John M. Cooper and D.S. Hutchinson (eds.), Cambridge: Hackett Publishing Company.
Plotinus (1991), *The Enneads*, Stephen MacKenna (trans.), London: Penguin.
Rorty, Richard (1980), *Philosophy and the Mirror of Nature*, Princeton, NJ: Princeton University Press.
——— (1982), "Philosophy as a Kind of Writing: An Essay on Derrida," in *Consequences of Pragmatism*, Minneapolis, MN: University of Minnesota Press.
——— (1999), "Religion as Conversation-stopper," in *Philosophy and Social Hope*, London: Penguin Books.
Russell, Bertrand (1946), *History of Western Philosophy*, London: George Allen and Unwin Ltd.
——— (1953a), "A Free Man's Worship," in *Mysticism and Logic*, London: Penguin.
——— (1953b), *Satan in the Suburbs*, New York: Simon and Schuster.
——— (1954), *Nightmares of Eminent Persons*, London: Bodley Head.
——— (1956), "Knowledge and Wisdom," in *Portraits from Memory, and Other Essays*, New York: Simon and Schuster.
——— (1959), *The Problems of Philosophy*, Oxford: Oxford University Press.

——— (1962), "The Pursuit of Truth," in *Fact and Fiction*, New York: Simon and Schuster.
——— (1972), "The Philosophy of Logical Atomism," in David Pears (ed.), *Russell's Logical Atomism*, London: Collins.
——— (1975), *The Autobiography of Bertrand Russell*, London: Allen and Unwin.
——— (2004), *Why I am not a Christian*, London: Routledge.
Samuels, Ernest (1979), *Bernard Berenson: The Making of a Connoisseur*, Cambridge, MA: Harvard University Press.
Searle, John (1975), "The Logical Status of Fictional Discourse," *New Literary History*, 6(2), pp. 319–332.
Seneca (1969), *Letters From a Stoic*, Robin Campbell (trans.), London: Penguin.
Shelley, Percy Bysshe (1992), "A Defense of Poetry," in Hazard Adams (ed.), *Critical Theory Since Plato*, New York: Harcourt, Brace, Javonovich.
Shusterman, Richard (1982), "Aesthetic Blindness to Textual Visuality," *Journal of Aesthetics and Art Criticism*, 41(1), pp. 87–96.
——— (1988), *T.S. Eliot and the Philosophy of Criticism*, New York: Columbia University Press.
——— (1994), "Eliot as Philosopher," in A.D. Moody (ed.), *The Cambridge Companion to* T.S. Eliot, Cambridge: Cambridge University Press, pp. 31–47.
——— (1997), *Practicing Philosophy: Pragmatism and the Philosophical Life*, London: Routledge.
——— (2000), *Surface and Depth*, Ithaca, NY: Cornell University Press.
——— (2008), *Body Consciousness: A Philosophy of Mindfulness and Somaesthetics*, Cambridge: Cambridge University Press.
——— (2012), *Thinking through the Body: Essays in Somaesthetics*, Cambridge: Cambridge University Press.
——— (2016), *The Adventures of the Man in Gold: Paths Between Art and Life*, Paris: Hermann.
——— (2017a), "The Philosopher without Words: Philosophy as Performative Art with *L'homme en Or*," in Curtis L. Carter (ed.), *Unsettled Boundaries: Philosophy, Art, Ethics East/West*, Milwaukee: Marquette University Press, pp. 36–50.
——— (2017b), "Somaesthetics and Self-Cultivation in Chinese Art," in E. Fischer-Lichte and B. Wihstutz (ed.), *Transformative Aesthetics*, London: Routledge, pp. 83–109.
——— (2021a), *Ars Erotica: Sex and Somaesthetics in the Classical Arts of Love*, Cambridge: Cambridge University Press.
——— (2021b), "Aesthetic Experience at the Borders of Art and Life: The Case of the Man in Gold," *Eidos: A Journal for Philosophy of Culture*, 5(2), pp. 103–111.
Sidney, Philip (1970), *An Apology for Poetry*, Englewood Cliffs, NJ: Prentice Hall.
Simonsen, Peter (2007), *Wordsworth and Word-Preserving Arts: Typgraphic Inscription, Ekphrasis and Posterity in the Later Work*, London: Palgrave Macmillan.
Sophocles (2011), *Oedipus Rex*, David Mulroy (trans.), Madison, WI: The University of Wisconsin Press.
Sullivan, Michael (1974), *The Three Perfections: Chinese Painting and Calligraphy*, London: Thames and Hudson.
Surya, Michel (2002), *Georges Bataille: An Intellectual Bibliography*, K. Filjalkowski and M. Richardson (trans.), London: Verso.

Thoreau, Henry David (1965), *Walden and Other Writings*, New York: The Modern Library.

Watson, Burton (trans.) (1968), *The Complete Works of Chuang Tsu*, New York: Columbia University Press.

Wittgenstein, Ludwig (1961), *Tractatus, Logico-Philosophicus*, D.F. Pears and B.F. McGuinness (trans.), London: Routledge.

——— (1967), *Letters from Ludwig Wittgenstein, with a Memoir by Paul Engelmann*, B. F. McGuinness (ed.), Oxford: Blackwell.

——— (1980), *Vermischte Bemerkungen/Culture and Value*, G.H. Von Wright (ed.), Oxford: Blackwell.

Wood, Alan (1957), *Bertrand Russell: The Passionate Skeptic*, London: Routledge.

Woolf, Virginia (2002), *The Common Reader: First Series*, Andrew McNeillie (ed.), Boston, MA: Mariner Books

Wordsworth, William (1814), *The Poetical Works of William Wordsworth*, William Knight (ed.), London: Macmillan and Co., Ltd.

——— (1949), *The Poetical Works of William Wordsworth*, vol. 4, E. De Selincourt and Helen Darbishire (eds.), Oxford: Clarendon Press.

——— (1977), "The Prelude," in J.C. Maxwell (ed.), *A Parallel Text*, New Haven, CT: Yale University Press.

Xenophon (1990), "Memoirs of Socrates," in H. Tredennick and R. Waterfield (trans.), *Conversations of Socrates*, London: Penguin.

Index

absence 72–4, 91n9
abstraction 50–1
abyss 67, 71–3, 82
actions 12–13, 33
aesthetics 9, 23, 47, 51, 64–5
affect/feeling x, 18–19, 50, 60–1, 80–1, 83, 101–2, 115–17
alienation 24, 55
ambiguity 43–4, 71–3
Ambrose, Saint 25
amusement: as value for literature 5, 7, 78–9
anguish 71
Apollodorus 8
Arendt, Hannah 19, 92
Aristotle 6, 101
assertion: asserting/vs showing 7–9, 84, 90
attention 18, 35, 52, 59–61, 69, 106; *see also* consciousness
Augustine, Saint xi, 24, 25–33, 39, 40, 47, 50, 55, 92
author 29–30, 37–8, 41, 45, 49, 51–3, 55, 68, 70–1, 79, 80–1
autobiography 15, 20, 28–9, 38, 46, 81
autonomy 2–3, 22n15

Bacon, Francis 7, 8, 11
balance 98, 104
Bataille, Georges xi, 58, 59–67, 69, 75, 90, 91n4, 91n7, 92
Beardsley, Monroe 7
beauty 2, 23–4, 30, 95, 108
Beauvoir, Simone de 19–20, 92
being 16–17, 19, 23–4, 27–8, 33, 35–7, 50–1, 72–4, 77–8, 91n9
Blanchot, Maurice xi, 6, 58, 59, 67–74, 75, 90
body 13–14, 35, 65, 99–100; Chinese conception of 98–100, 103–4, 108–9, 110, 118n4; cultivation of 92–3
Bradley, F.H. 58
brushstroke 95–96, 108, 118n12

Cahill, James 102
calligraphy 94–5, 100–5, 116–17; somatic dimensions of 94–6, 98–100, 118n4, 118n10
Catherine, Saint 17
Cavell, Stanley 21n8
change 29–30, 37, 42, 45, 50, 60, 64, 82
Chinese philosophy 13, 92–4, 98, 108
Christianity 17, 25–6, 47, 51, 53–4
Cicero 12, 25
Coleridge, Samuel T. 40
communication 38–9, 52–3, 58–62, 64, 80
computer 116–17, 117n1
concealment 18, 54–5, 63–4, 79, 87, 116
concept/the conceptual 1, 10–11, 13, 15–16, 43, 50–1, 59, 62, 67, 69, 102–3
Confucianism 13, 15, 92–3, 95, 97, 100, 102, 114–15
Confucius 13, 15, 92, 93
consciousness 29, 37, 41, 44, 46, 52, 59–66, 73, 79–80
consistency 24, 36–8, 90
contemplation 2, 17, 80, 83, 106–9
continuity 63, 65–6, 75
conversation 16, 55
creation 3, 20, 23, 30, 41, 44–6, 72, 98, 101

Danto, Arthur 8–9
Daoism 13, 93, 115–16

death 14, 23, 28, 31–3, 47, 60, 64–7, 70–7, 82–3, 86–9, 91n9
Derrida, Jacques 9
desire 4, 23–5, 35–6, 61, 65, 82, 84, 86–7
despair 28–9, 82, 89
Dewey, John 13, 16
dialogue 1, 3–6, 8, 12, 26, 33–4, 54, 69
Diogenes, Laertius 12, 15
Donne, John 75
doubt 14, 24, 43, 86, 89
drama 2, 4–5, 11, 25, 65
duality 36, 40

ecstasy 60, 62, 64–7, 77, 81–2
Eliot, T.S. xi, 58, 59, 75–81, 82, 90, 91n15, 92, 117, 117n1
Eliot, Vivienne 58
emancipation 61–2, 66–8, 71–2, 247–8
embodiment 11–20, 35, 46, 51, 70, 92–4, 103
emotion 6, 45, 60, 68, 80, 87, 93, 98
emptiness 68, 71–3, 75, 115
energy 64, 92; in Chinese writing 94–100, 102, 104–5, 110; *see also* qi
Engelmann, Paul 56
Epictetus 12, 24
Epicurus 14, 15
eroticism 59, 65–7
essay (genre) 32–33
eternity 44, 66
ethics 9–10, 14, 50–1, 85, 92, 101
evil 17, 28, 32, 43, 63, 67, 82–4, 86, 88
existence 24, 48–9, 50–7, 58–9, 60–6, 67–73, 75–7, 80

fallacies 87–8
fallibilism 78, 80, 87
family 26, 34, 36, 39, 58, 92
feelings 18, 20, 28–9, 32, 40, 45–7, 49–51, 60–1, 65, 69, 74, 80–1, 83, 85, 90, 93–4, 96–8, 101–2, 104, 109, 115–17
feminine 3–4, 19–20
fiction 1, 7, 26, 31, 39, 53, 56, 58, 63–5, 67, 69–73, 79, 83–4, 89–90
finitude/infinitude 44, 50, 55
flexibility 37–8, 78
flux 64, 67, 77–8
Fong, Wen C. 96, 110, 112, 119n16
form 2, 5, 14, 20, 23, 38, 43, 68, 71, 74
Foucault, Michel 13, 17–18, 20
Franklin, Benjamin 96
freedom 33, 55, 65, 82

gender 4, 21n3
God 17, 26–32, 47, 50, 55, 82
Goethe, Johann Wolfgang von 17, 19
grace 17, 27, 55, 95, 106

Habermas, Jürgen 16
habits 101, 104–5
Hadot, Pierre 13
happiness 2, 5, 14, 33, 67
harmony 2, 16, 26, 37, 64, 77, 91n7, 92–3, 99, 103, 106–108
health 17, 23–4, 27, 48, 53, 56n5, 93
Hegel, Georg Wilhelm Friedrich 50, 58
Heidegger, Martin 91n9
history 6, 8, 41, 46, 101
Holderlin, Friedrich 69
Homer 3
Huang, Gongwang 103, 112
human nature 13–14, 36–7, 86
humility 16, 34, 55, 77–9
Hutchinson, Mary 39

ideality 50–2, 78
illusion 10, 51–4, 115
imagination 7, 10–11, 34, 79, 83
immediacy 50–1, 62–3, 65
immortality 18, 23, 46, 73
indirection 52–3, 79
individuation 63–4, 72
induction 87–8
ineffability 52, 56, 58ff., 77
ink 94–6, 98–101
ink wash painting 96, 105–6, 110–11, 114, 118n9
inner experience 19, 50–1, 59–66
interpretation 4, 30, 85–6

James, William 13, 60
Jocasta 17

Kant, Immanuel 17
Keats, John 41
Kierkegaard, Michael 47
Kierkegaard, Peter 48
Kierkegaard, Søren xi, 8, 13, 18, 24, 47–56, 57n14, 57n15, 57n16, 59, 67, 92
knowledge 2–4, 6, 15, 27, 59–62, 77–8, 82, 86–90

La Boétie, Étienne de 32–4, 36
language x; discursive 60–2; inadequacy/difficulty/limitation of metaphor 4, 9–10, 51, 77, 79;

literal vs literary 9; ordinary language 7, 10, 56, 59, 60, 62, 68–9, 83, 90; phonetic 94; versus poetry 6–7
Laozi 116
Levinas, Emmanuel 67
limit experience 59, 67
literature: and eroticism 65–7; and existence 72–4; as linguistically different and derivative 7–11; and mystical experience 60; space of 70–3; and wisdom 79–80
loneliness 32, 53, 75–6, 81–2, 106, 115
love 26–8, 30–2, 42, 82

Marcus Aurelius 24, 56n1
meaning, lack of 3, 6, 8–9, 13–14, 19–20, 27, 30–1, 38, 40, 43–6, 52, 54, 61–2, 65–6, 68–9, 71–2, 75–9, 81–2, 90, 96, 102, 104, 116–17
measure 26
meditation 27, 31, 110, 115–16
meliorism 12, 13, 15, 18, 20, 47, 100
memory 4, 18, 29, 33, 38, 46
Mencius 92
metaphysics 2, 9, 14, 26, 43, 76
Milton, John 11, 39
mimesis 2
mind 6, 27, 33–7, 41–2, 44–6, 55, 81–2, 98, 104, 115–16
moderation 3, 24, 118n5
Montaigne, Michel de xi, 7, 12, 15, 17, 24, 32–9, 46, 47, 55, 56n5, 90, 92, 97–8
mood 94–5, 97–8, 101–5, 110
muses 3, 7
music 26, 45, 93, 100, 108
mystical, the 59–63

nature 13–14, 17, 41–4, 46–7, 106–8
negation 69–70, 72
Ni, Zan 102–3, 105, 111–13, 118n12, 119n16
Nietzsche, Friedrich 9–10, 13, 15, 17, 18, 58, 64, 69
nonsense 8, 66
nothingness 68, 72–4
novel 20, 66

obscurity 68–9, 71–4, 81
Oedipus 17
Olsen, Regina (Kierkegaard's fiancé) 48
ontology 30, 41, 45, 77, 91n9, 115; *see also* metaphysics
oral composition 1, 5–6, 21n4, 43, 45, 53, 78, 94, 116
order 16, 24, 26–9, 34–8, 45, 64, 78, 94, 97, 103–4

pain 14, 17, 55, 60, 65–6
painting 94–5; *see also* ink wash painting
Pan, Gongkai 105
paradox 27–8, 49, 52, 56, 57n15, 58, 60, 69, 84
passion 38, 42, 49–52, 65–7, 81–2, 89
pattern 36, 38–9, 77, 116
Paul, Saint 36
peace 81, 85, 115–16
pederasty 3–4
pen 31, 94–6, 116
philosophical life x–xii, 12, 14, 17, 20, 22n15, 23–4, 27, 32–3, 41–2, 47–51, 105; aesthetic model 23; health model 23–4, 56n1
philosophy: academic and professional 16–17; as an art of living 13–15, 22n15, 23–4; and definition 1–2; as distinct from literature 5–6; genres of hegemony of 6; and knowledge 1; and language x, 6, 11; professionalization of 16–17, 39; quarrel with poetry 1; and truth 8–9; and wisdom x, 2, 11–12, 16, 77–9, 82–3, 92
Pittacus 16
Plato 1–6, 11, 14, 21n3, 23, 92, 116
pleasure 2, 4, 6–7, 11, 14, 24, 26, 31, 35–7, 39, 61, 65–7, 79, 108
Plotinus 24
poet/poetry 1–7, 10–11, 26–7, 39–46, 49, 56, 59–60, 62, 63, 65–6, 70, 77–81, 91n7, 93–4, 100–2, 106, 117
poiesis 6, 101
politics 24, 47, 100
possession 3–4, 21n3, 81
practice 6, 12–16, 101
print 43–4, 47, 78, 116
pseudonym 18, 52–4, 57n14
Pythagoras 51

qi (energy) 92, 95–6, 98–9

reading 13, 19, 21n4, 25, 29, 38, 45, 55, 79, 115
reality 2, 4, 6, 27, 50, 56, 59, 63, 65, 68–72, 74–7, 81
reason 10, 24, 26, 33–5, 56n5, 59, 63, 88
refinement 13, 75, 93, 95, 98, 100, 103

reflection 94, 100, 105–110, 114–16
religion 25, 58, 60, 91n14
rhetoric 2, 25–6,
Rimbaud, Arthur 65
ritual 47, 93, 97
Rorty, Richard 9, 16
Russell, Bertrand xi, 58–9, 81–90, 90n3, 91n12, 91n14, 91n15, 92

sage 92–3, 99, 104
Sartre, Jean-Paul 20
Schiller, Friedrich 47
science 8–10, 21n8, 22n15, 89
Searle, John 7, 8
Sebond, Raymond 32
self: self-cultivation 15, 17–18, 36, 41, 92–3, 95–6, 100–12, 114, 117; self-examination 11, 16, 19, 35, 48, 95–6, 103, 108, 112, 114; self-knowledge 11–12, 16–18, 24, 27–9, 33–5, 41, 47–8, 92, 103–5; unity of 24, 26–9, 36–8, 42, 45, 49, 64–5
Seneca 12, 15
sensation 19, 35, 41, 67
sense 11, 62, 64–5
sex 3–4, 25, 65–7
Sextus Empiricus 90
Shakespeare, William 11, 39
Shelley, Percy Bysshe 10–11
Shen, Zhou 105, 114–16
Sidney, Sir Phillip 7
signs 9, 43, 72
silence 51, 54–5, 61, 74, 77–8, 115, 118n5, 119n20
skepticism 33, 81–90
society 12, 20, 47, 93
Socrates 1–3, 11–12, 14, 17, 23, 33, 48–9
somaesthetics 13–15, 93, 98–100, 103, 106, 117
soul 2, 4, 14, 17–18, 23–4, 26–7, 35–6, 37, 48, 56n5, 80
sound 31, 43, 108, 115–16
speech 1, 5–6, 16; speech acts 7–8
style 94–6, 101–2, 104–5, 117, 118n4
subjectivity 18–19, 50, 52, 55, 68
symbol 69–70, 72–3, 84–7, 97, 110

Tao, Yuanming 109
technology 5–6, 116–17
text 5, 18, 21n4, 24, 30, 33, 43, 45–6, 53–5, 78
theology 22n15, 25, 32, 48
Thoreau, Henry David 13
thought 6, 19, 31, 33–4, 36, 42, 50, 73, 82, 115–17
three perfections, the xi, 95, 102
time 29–30, 38, 59, 76–8, 91n7
tradition 2, 18, 25, 92–3, 95–7, 101–2, 104–5
tranquility 39, 56n5, 104
travel/wandering 39–40, 44, 46
truth 8–11, 15, 20, 26–8, 46, 48–53, 55–6, 59–60, 71–2, 86–90
type (and type/token distinction) 43–46
typewriter 117

Uhland, Ludwig 56
unity 16, 24, 27, 29, 36–8, 42, 49, 62–6; primal 64
universality 6, 8, 15
universe 13, 26, 44, 65, 69, 82, 96
utility 11, 15, 63

value 5–6, 8, 12–15, 19, 24, 63, 68, 82, 89, 101
Varnhagen, Rahel 19
violence 59, 65–7, 83
Virgil 25
virtue 3–4, 12, 15, 23–4, 30, 32–3, 37, 42, 78, 82, 92–3, 96, 118n5
visuality 43, 45, 95–6, 101–2
void 72–4, 76

Wang, Meng 103, 105, 107
Wang, Yu 103
Webster, John 75
Wei, Shuo 99
wholeness 37, 42–6, 48, 71; *see also* unity
will 36, 50, 52, 61, 73, 104, 115–16
wisdom x–xi, 2–3, 11, 16, 23, 27, 35, 37, 77–80, 82–3, 92
Wittgenstein, Ludwig 8–9, 55, 56, 90
woman 3–4, 19–20, 69–70
Woolf, Virginia 96
words 6, 13, 25–6, 29–31, 37–8, 43, 45–6, 51, 68–9, 75–7, 79–80, 119n20
Wordsworth, Dorothy 39
Wordsworth, William xi, 24, 39–47, 92
writing 4–6, 9–10, 18–20, 26, 29–35, 37–9, 42–9, 52–3, 55, 58–9, 68, 71, 91n10, 92–5, 98–105, 115–17, 117n1, 117n2, 118n4; and the art of living 23–32; and reshaping the self 34–6; and self-examination/

self-knowledge 12, 16–19, 33, 35, 53, 95–6, 98, 103–4, 108, 110, 112, 117; and self-transformation 17–18, 20, 29; ontological complexity of 43–7
Wu, Zhen 105, 109

Xenophon 12, 14
Xie, He 99
Xunzi 92

Zhuangzi 93, 99, 100